Real World
CAREER
DEVELOPMENT
STRATEGIES

That

Insight Publishing Company
Sevierville, Tennessee

Real World
CAREER DEVELOPMENT STRATEGIES
That
WORK

Published by,
Insight Publishing Company
PO Box 4189
Sevierville, TN 37862

Printed in the United States of America

Senior Editor, Russ Hollingsworth
Copy Editor, Mitch Moore
Concept Editor, Chris Hollingsworth

ISBN 1-885640-90-0

Table Of Contents

A Message From The Publisher

Some of my most rewarding experiences in business—or in my personal life, for that matter—have been at meetings, conventions or gatherings, after the formal events have concluded. Inevitably, small groups of ten to fifteen men and women gather together to rehash the happenings of the day and to exchange war stories, recently heard jokes or the latest gossip from their industry. It is in these informal gatherings where some of the best lessons can be learned.

Usually, in informal groups of professionals, there are those who clearly have lived through more battles and learned more lessons than others. These are the men and women who are really getting the job done, and everyone around the room knows it. When they comment on the topic of the moment, they don't just spout the latest hot theory or trend, and they don't ramble on and on without a relevant point. These battle-scarred warriors have lessons to share that everyone senses are just a little more real, more relevant and therefore, worthy of more attention.

These are the kind of people we have recruited for the Power Learning series of books. Each title offers contributions from men and women who are making a significant impact on their culture, in their field, and on their colleagues and clients. This edition offers a variety of themes in the area of Career Development Strategies. It is ripe with "the good stuff," as an old friend of mine used to always say. Inside these pages you'll find ideas, insights, strategies and philosophies that are working with real people, in real companies and under real circumstances.

It is our hope that you keep this book with you until you've dog-eared every chapter and made so many notes in the margins that you have trouble seeing the original words on the pages. There is treasure here. Enjoy digging!

Russ Hollingsworth

Chapter 1

Fit For Life—Aligning Your Career With Your Life Purpose

Anita Schamber, Ed.D.

What does it mean to have a good career fit? In the career development field, this refers to the match between a person's life purpose, values, abilities and talents and the requirements of his job or career. Sometimes it is easier to determine the right career fit for people other than ourselves. Few of us can imagine Mother Teresa as a forest ranger, Tiger Woods as an opera star or Martha Stewart as a ballerina. These celebrities simply don't fit the careers beyond those for which they are (were) obviously gifted.

When your own career fit is not so obvious, you may fall into the trap of believing that if you simply work hard enough, you can follow any career path you want. In his book *Why You Can't Be Anything You Want to Be*, Arthur Miller dispels the myth that hard work alone opens the door to achieving whatever one desires. The reason this is untrue, Miller points out, is because we have been uniquely designed or "hard-wired" by our Creator with particular motivations and talents to fulfill a specific purpose on earth. Miller would argue that when we are tuned in to our purpose, passion and particular talents, we will be able to discern possible career fields more readily.

A second trap to finding a career fit lies in the distorted pictures of success promoted in the popular culture. When comedian Phyllis Diller was in her late thirties, she worked as a scrub woman to earn a meager income. At the time, she concluded that to be successful, she had to be beautiful and rich. Naturally, her self-assessment indicated that she didn't measure up to those two standards. Then one day as she was cleaning up the trash, she found a discarded book by Claude Bristol, *The Magic of Believing*, which transformed her thinking. Bristol advised his readers to believe in themselves and to put their best talents to work for them. Diller's outstanding gift was her offbeat humor, which made people laugh spontaneously. Ultimately it was her belief in her talents—not her appearance or wealth—that led to her success as a comedian.

If we must overcome artificial barriers set by our culture, how can we know when we have a good career fit? Clues often show up in early childhood. Reflecting upon my own preschool days, I enjoyed playing in the make-believe world of Cinderella. Surprisingly, I didn't choose the role of the main character, whose stepmother required her to clean up cinders and ashes around the fireplace. Rather, I was enchanted by the role of the fairy godmother, whose magic wand changed the lives of everyone it touched, including Cinderella's.

My childhood games planted the seeds and nourished my current passion and talent for serving as a life/career coach. My purpose and calling as a coach is first to inspire, motivate, encourage and equip others to achieve their God-given purposes in life. Second, I encourage a program of life/career "fitness" to help my clients create sustainable opportunities in a changing world (more on that later). It's no surprise that the symbol of my passion for touching lives—a gold, quilted, star-shaped wand—occupies a prominent place on my desk.

Stop for a minute and look back on your life. Can you identify traces of your present passion, talents or values that showed up in your childhood activities? Have career myths created obstacles to either identifying or using your best talents? What kind of plan have you created to keep your career viable?

In this chapter, I hope to start you out on the road toward aligning your career with your life purpose, passion, particular talents and values. Doing so requires that you treat your life and your career as if they were living organisms in need of achieving and maintaining physical fitness. In other words, for your life and career to fit, they must first *be* fit.

One of the most effective ways to achieve this kind of fitness is by working with your own personal life/career coach. If you're not familiar with the work of these life strategists, this chapter will explain how you can benefit from a coach and where to find one to work with well.

Even if you're not quite ready for a life/career coach, you'll find some exercises and assessments at the end of this chapter that are often used by coaches in helping their clients determine their ideal life/career matches. Working through them on your own will help you take a giant step toward ensuring that your aspirations and your job are fit for life.

LIFE/CAREER FITNESS

Most people know what physical fitness is, but what about life/career fitness? I have found that the fitness metaphor is appropriate for describing the essential process of ensuring your career sustainability in an ever-changing world.

To avoid deceiving you, however, let me first share my personal experiences with physical fitness. Although I wanted to maintain a slim, fit body, I was never swept away by the physical fitness craze or jogging mania. In fact, I couldn't find one good reason for sweating and straining for forty-five minutes in the name of exercise. As a result, I declined invitations to join my friends, who trekked off to the local gym three to five times a week. Unlike them, I refused to buy into the mantra of "no pain, no gain." (Fitness experts insist this is a big lie anyway; being fit and healthy doesn't require that you hurt!)

While my friends worked with personal trainers to build muscles or upper body strength, reduce body fat or contour their ordinary bodies into fantastic temples, I encouraged and coached them from the sidelines. (At that time, this represented somewhat of a credibility gap as a coach, if I do say so myself!) On the one occasion I did slip down to the "Y" in my bulky sweatshirt and black tights, I felt dismayed to discover Ms. Bodybuilder USA—decked out in her modest, hot pink tights and tan, concave midriff—working out right next to me.

In those days, I needed someone like TV's talk show host, "Dr. Phil" to tell me to get up off my chair and into a workout program. Instead, I wasted years alternating between fit and flabby. Eventually, I bought a treadmill and began walking in the privacy of my own home to improve my personal fitness.

What does my persistent resistance to becoming physically fit have to do with your career? It highlights the fact that ninety percent of our behaviors are habitual. Therefore, we need to develop a fitness paradigm early in our lives, be it for our physical health or career well being. Track your daily patterns to identify your current life/work habits. How long have you maintained them? If you show no signs of serious discipline, ask yourself what it will take for you to change. If you don't exercise and work out, you will become physically flabby. Likewise, you can become "career flabby" in no time at all.

LIFE/CAREER COACHING

What does an Olympic athlete have that you don't have? Some of the answers are obvious—a gold, silver or bronze medal, not to mention the fame and endorsements that go along with outstanding athletic achievement. One of the most significant things that the Olympian has that most of us lack, however, is a good coach. While it's obvious why athletes work with coaches, *you* may not have discovered a need for one. In the next few pages, we'll explore life/career coaching as a relationship in which a professional helps people achieve fulfilling lives and careers.

A startling statistic illustrates why a life/career coach may be useful. Although adults spend between 80,000 and 100,000 hours working over a forty-year time period (ages twenty-five to sixty-five) and another 20,000 hours in the rat race commuting to and from work, only five to six percent spend any significant time focusing on life/career issues. While we acknowledge that our careers are extremely important and affect many other aspects of our lives—such as income, where we live, our neighbors and friends, amount of leisure time and key life experiences—we tend to spend more time deciding what car to buy, where to go on vacation or which great bargains to purchase on e-Bay.

If you are a fan of Dr. Phil's television show, you've probably heard him define insanity as doing the same things over and over, but expecting different results! In his book, *The Pathfinder*, Nicholas Lore reports that only ten percent of adults are operating at the highest level of career satisfaction. Such craziness applies to us when we postpone doing what we really are passionate about in our careers simply because it is easier *not* to change.

Even when we intend to follow our dreams, some of us end up settling for second best when setbacks occur. You may have promised yourself that when the time is right, the investments are secure, or the children are raised, you will change jobs or careers, go back to school or start your own business. Author Norman Cousins, who survived a near-fatal illness, noted, "Death is not the greatest loss in life. The greatest loss is what dies inside us while we live." How well are you living your dream?

Unfortunately, some people remain stuck in a holding pattern until they receive a wake-up call in the form of a life or career crisis. Others will join the club whose members are the most talented in the world, but whose talents no one enjoyed because they took them to the grave unused. The cemeteries are the final refuges for many would be artists, writers, politicians, pastors, architects and others who never followed their dreams to fulfillment.

As a reader of this book, you are among the exceptional minority who are taking steps to discover practical ideas and tools to plan more satisfying careers. From this important launching point, you may still discover that old habits die hard. This is where a life/career coach can help, someone who can help you break well-engrained patterns by holding you accountable for co-creating the life you want! Let's explore some basic questions about life/career coaching.

- What do we mean by "coaching?"
- How does a coach differ from a counselor, a manager, a supervisor or a good friend?
- What are some indications that you might benefit from working work with a coach?
- How do you choose the right coach? Can you afford one?
- How will you and a coach work together?
- What are the key questions to explore with a coach to achieve life/work fitness?

What is life/career coaching?

Your image of a coach may vary according to your experience. While some might think of an intense personality like basketball coach Bobby Knight, others picture the inspiring football coach Lou Holtz. In the movie *Remember the Titans*, the contrasting styles of the African American head football coach and his white assistant created obvious tensions as they created a winning football team out of a racially mixed group of guys. The coaches knew the team needed the best talents of both races to work together, but they disagreed on how to make it happen. However, these models from the athletic world fall short and can even distort the picture of a professional life/career coach.

In the dictionary, one definition of coach is "a vehicle for moving a person of value from one place to another." This immediately brings to mind the image of Queen Elizabeth II being carried in an elaborate horse-drawn carriage. In the same way, a life/career coach is a trained professional whose goal is to help someone of unique value to develop and change. Metaphorically speaking, the coach is the vehicle for moving that person to where he or she desires to be.

The International Coach Federation recognizes professional life/career coaching as "an ongoing partnership that helps clients produce fulfilling results in their personal and professional lives." Fran Fisher, president of the Academy of Coach Training, defines it as "a relationship of unconditional acceptance where learning, performance, growth and change naturally occur." In career coaching, the focus of the person being coached usually narrows to career issues, although coaches may help their clients analyze the issues within a holistic life context. By broadening the scope of coaching, the coach and client work on issues of balance and satisfaction between career and other domains, such as spiritual life, marriage, family relationships, finances, learning, leisure and community service.

A life/career coach partners with the client to achieve the results that he or she wants in life and work. The difference between struggling on your own and working with a coach is like the difference between buying a cheap suit off the rack and purchasing a custom-designed suit that fits to a tee. A good coach knows one size doesn't fit all. Instead, she considers her clients as the owners of their own agendas, helping them become clear about their goals, both short and long term. The coach brings expert knowledge about life and careers to the table, but honors those being coached as the experts on their own lives.

A personal experience illustrates the importance of the principle of honoring the client as responsible for his own life/career change. Recently I coached a highly creative gentleman who worked as a technologist in an information systems group in a medium-sized company. After a few coaching sessions, I could have easily made the mistake of assuming the role of expert in his life and begun pumping solutions into our coaching conversations. And because he had expressed his creative passions so vividly, my intuition would have been to redirect him toward a position which honored his talents in music, dance and the dramatic arts.

Although my instincts might have been accurate, my integrity as a coach required me to set my agenda aside and honor my client as the creator of his own future. Instead of a radical change, we developed a short-term plan that involved his finding a more creative position in the IT department. At the same time, he identified additional ways to engage his creative talents outside work. The client set a goal of moving into teaching dramatic arts in public schools. As he considered his life holistically, he was able to set a time line that matched other life events, including his wife's development of her home business and the entrance of his children into school. Because he took the responsibility for designing his future (while I remained a guide on the side), we have been able to celebrate his current job satisfaction and successes.

What can a coach do—and not do—for you?

It's important to understand how life/career coaches differ from other professionals.

Coaches are not therapists or counselors.

Therapists usually support clients who need to dig deeply into personal problems or areas of dysfunction in their lives. Counselors help clients focus on the causes of emotional pain or conflicts deeply rooted in their past. Coaches, in contrast, work with relatively healthy and stable individuals who choose to make changes in their present lives.

Career coaches are not consultants.

They don't have all the answers, although they are hired for their expertise in the career development field. The life/career coach has special knowledge and skills in career assessments, career planning and development, and career transition areas but refrains from being an expert on your life or your career aspirations. You alone hold that knowledge and potential. The career coach willingly walks alongside you as you discover, plan or make changes in life or career directions.

Coaches are not mentors.

They do have skills that are similar to mentors, but a mentor is usually an older or more experienced expert who has walked the path of life experience that the protégé wants to learn. He or she is expected to give advice, teach and otherwise guide his protégé into higher levels of excellence.

A couple of other notes about the responsibilities of life/career coaches:

- Coaches are not in your chain of command if you seek coaching within an organization. While managers may use coaching skills with their employees, they also must support the mission and goals of the organization. Your desire to change jobs or careers and to develop skills that will make you marketable outside your current position may not be compatible with the business strategy of your work unit.
- A coach cannot be your relative or even your best friend, even though he or she may be your personal champion. You may have had parents who played an important role in shaping your life/career choices as you grew up. If you were lucky,

they offered a listening ear rather than hand out liberal advice as to what was best for you. But many parents *do* think they know what is best and push their children along a chosen path—theirs. Years later, as adults, these children may discover that what was best at one time no longer is, and they may feel trapped in a totally mismatched vocation.

A dramatic case in point is a pediatrician who recognized that he had entered medicine to please his parents and to fulfill their dreams for him rather than his dreams for himself. After he had been in practice a few years, he had to fight the mental gremlins that reminded him of how much money and time he had invested in becoming a doctor and how disappointed his parents would be if he left the medical field. At the same time, he acknowledged his overwhelming passion for working with adults and his desire to spend more time with his own young children— both honorable goals. These personal priorities, coupled with his awareness of the numbers of physicians leaving medical practice, prompted this doctor to enroll in a career development certification program. His preparation opened the door for him to become a successful career coach to—you guessed it—other disgruntled doctors and nurses who were leaving the medical field to find their own new careers!

What are some indications that you might benefit from working with a coach?

The outcome of effective coaching is change, which can range from minimal, behavioral changes to transformational life changes that occur over time. Therefore, your first instinct to hire a coach may occur when you actively seek change in your life or career, particularly when you feel stuck and can't seem to get out of a rut on your own. One of my executive clients, who was in a senior position of leadership in her organization, appeared in my office wound up like the Energizer® bunny, continuously on the run. She was showing signs of fatigue, depression and low self-regard. We worked together to identify priorities for her life, including taking time out for periods of rest and reflection. When she committed to developing a healthier life style, she developed a plan to break her old habit of staying in work mode around the clock. She created small steps for short-term change and larger goals for permanent change.

You can probably see the benefit of working with a coach if you are trying to change from one career to another. But there is a host of other life/career situations that may likewise signal the need for a coach:

- When you are exploring many career paths but are not sure which one will make the most of your talents and interests
- When you have lost passion for your job or otherwise feel ill at ease in your current work situation but can't decide why
- When too many people who claim to know what's best for you keep telling you what you should be doing, and your voice is getting lost in the crowd
- When you're trying to discover what you want to be when you grow up—and you are already forty years old
- When you've recognized a pattern in your life of settling for second best and are now ready to "go for the gold"
- When you feel stuck or locked into your job by golden handcuffs such as great compensation and benefits
- When you know what you want but are afraid to go after it without support because the challenges associated with change seem so formidable
- When you don't see clear choices because you are only partially sighted and need another trained perspective
- When life/career issues are out of balance
- When you know what you're good at but have never fully developed your talents
- When you feel like you are trying to balance a number of priorities, just one of which is your career
- When you have a good plan but fail to follow through
- When the urgent demands on your life drain your energy for doing the truly important things
- When you are in search of increased meaning, satisfaction or value at your current stage of life
- When you're too young to retire but are ready to "reformat" your career
- When your job ends suddenly or rumors abound concerning impending layoffs in your company
- When you find yourself facing an unexpected life transition
- When the world seems to have changed but you have not
- When you simply need a neutral sounding board for your thoughts

How can you select a good career coach?

After you identify a need for a coach, the next challenge is to find one with whom you can work well. While you could pick someone randomly from the phone book, the partnership you hope to form is important enough to require more diligent research. Second only to a spouse, this person will be part of your life experience, sharing your dreams, fears, hopes, needs, wins and losses in both your personal and professional lives. Therefore, having a coach whom you can trust is essential. Well-trained professionals who hold credentials in the areas of coaching, career development and human development are a good place to start. Coaches, who are certified by the International Coach Federation, have been evaluated as having appropriate training, experience, and ethics to serve in a professional capacity.

In addition, trained life/career coaches exhibit qualities and practices that set them apart from others. A good coach:

- Creates an environment which makes you feel at ease
- Establishes rapport with you easily
- Seems to be genuinely interested in you
- Spends sufficient time getting to know you during an initial interview
- Expresses values that are compatible with yours
- Openly describes his/her coaching approach with you
- Doesn't purport to have all the answers
- Will maintain confidentiality
- Provides references or comes recommended by clients
- Provides evidence of his expertise, training and credentials
- Charges fees commensurate with the services provided

If you choose to hire a coach, it is important to do some comparison shopping. By interviewing two or three candidates, you can compare and contrast their qualities and ultimately choose the one with whom you feel most compatible. While you are sizing up a coach, she/he will also be assessing you as well. By asking questions about your background, needs and wishes and listening to your responses, the prospective coach will determine how coachable you are, as well as how committed you are to working toward goals you set.

In the initial interview, the coach will introduce herself to you, explain her coaching philosophy and practice, clarify expectations of how you will work together and explain the fee schedule for services. In many cases, a coach will offer a complimentary session so you can get a feel for the typical coaching experience. Otherwise, fees can range from a hundred to several hundred dollars per hour.

If the two of you agree to pursue coaching together, you will write many of the co-created decisions into a contract, which you both will sign.

How will you and the coach work together?

A good career coach always adheres to important principles and ethical considerations in working with clients. The nine listed below are essential to a healthy coaching relationship:

- The Principle of Respect: The coach treats the person being coached respectfully, honoring his or her dignity.
- The Principle of Safety/Confidentiality: The coach provides a "safety zone" by offering unconditional acceptance. This allows those being coached to be themselves, provides them with a sounding board and gives them space to risk exploring ideas or making mistakes. The coach maintains confidence regarding the content and outcome of each session.
- The Principle of Honoring the Client's Agenda: The coach honors the need or focus of the client rather than his own agenda. He does not determine what the person being coached needs or try to steer her in that direction. (Exception: The coach will, from time to time, use career tools and suggestions to assist the client.)
- The Principle of Relevance: The coach serves as pathfinder in facilitating focus on the relevant priorities the client identifies.
- The Principle of Empowerment: The coach views those being coached as having the capacity to find their own answers to their life/career questions. The coach facilitates the process of discovery.
- The Principles of Clarity, Alignment, Action: The coach facilitates clarity of the client's life/career issues—helping her to align her goals or intentions with possible actions—and then supports her in taking action. The coach asks questions to raise awareness and help the client to make decisions about her job and/or life.
- The Principle of Wholeness: The coach promotes wholeness and physical, mental, emotional and spiritual balance ("hurry sickness" and overload are symptoms of an out-of-balance life).
- The Principle of Facilitating Process: The coach focuses on the client's learning process as well as the results The coach

values the quality of the person's journey and the value of learning to make change meaningful.

- The Principle of Language: As a person thinks, so he becomes. The coach promotes the use of empowering language and attitudes so that the person being coached becomes healthy, responsible and confident rather than weak and stuck. A coach uses language which is, for the most part, honoring, positive and powerful. A coach may also have to confront a client's erroneous thinking by asking powerful questions which unmask the source of his crippling belief systems.

The coach should reflect these principles from the first interview until the fulfillment of the coaching contract.

I am often asked what the coaching sessions themselves are like. Think of them as well developed conversations. Depending on what your career questions are, the coach will have an array of methods and tools that she can use to help you determine your passion, assess your talents, gifts and values, create an action plan, overcome obstacles and move forward. A quick look into the coach's tool kit will reveal:

- Assessment tools that include the MBTI (Myers Briggs Type Indicator), Strong Vocational Interest Inventory, the Birkman, SIMA(Systematic Inventory of Motivated Abilities), Values Inventories and others to help collect personal data important to your future
- An analysis of gaps in competencies that differentiates those required from those you need to develop
- Goal-setting tools for the short and long term
- Powerful questions and inquiries for deep reflection
- Action assignments for getting information
- Interviewing skills that are sharply focused
- Models and tools for writing up-to-date resumes
- Job-hunting tools and activities for exploring the labor market
- Networking with multiple links in your future
- Dialogues and decision making
- Action planning

While you may mentally fight the notion, a good coach often encourages you to explore outside your comfort zone, to test new ideas and choices, and to risk in ways you wouldn't dare do without a support system. The coach often holds your feet to the fire, becoming your accountability partner as you set and achieve small steps en route to larger goals.

By the way, another source of support you might put at your disposal is a "personal board of directors." I recommend that you create this board by sharing your goals and action plan with a small, carefully-selected group of friends, business colleagues, church associates and people from your professional network. Ask each to act as a peer coach by investing time with you over a designated period, holding you accountable for taking incremental steps toward your goal and celebrating your accomplishments and milestones along the way. By checking in with these cheerleaders on a weekly or monthly basis, you will find it easier to move forward in maximizing your plan for maintaining life/career fitness.

To find out more about life/career coaching, check the references in the appendix of this book. Or you can consult the International Coach Federation, Coachville Inc., The Institute for Life Coaching, the Christian Coaches Network, any accredited coach training institution or this author for more information about this growing field.

Now that you understand the basic concept of life/career coaching, you will be able to apply it more fully to your own circumstances. As you can see, you don't have to be an Olympic athlete to work with a coach, and you *can* be the winner of a more satisfying, productive and meaningful life and career. As a first step, you might want to complete the following exercises and surveys, which are typical of the kinds of tools that a coach might use to help you assess your specific life and career issues. It is my hope that through them you will gain clarity about your passions, needs, intentions and actions.

A LIFE/CAREER FITNESS ASSESSMENT

A good career fit depends on the continuous exercise of life/career processes. As a career coach, I discern my clients' commitment to their careers through a quick assessment. I ask them these questions:

- What new knowledge or skills have you added or developed in the last six months?
- What new self-understanding have you gained in the same period?
- Looking at your life as a whole, in which areas are you experiencing high levels of satisfaction? Low levels of satisfaction? (Categories can include marriage, family,

finances, personal health, emotional, spiritual, leisure, community, service, work and education.)
- If you were to make one significant change in your life, what would it be?

These questions provide critical information regarding the career health of my clients. If they aren't learning something new, they are falling behind the curve because of the acceleration of change and the demand for continuous learning. Currently, the shelf life of knowledge is only three to six months. After that time, a gap begins growing between what we know and what we need to know to stay current in our respective fields.

THE LIFE/CAREER FITNESS MODEL

Stephen Covey popularized the notion of "beginning with the end in mind." So start by asking yourself what a satisfying career would look like. The first creation of your future is in your mind. What will it take to create that future? The second creation is the realization of the outcome you want. It is important to realize that most career changes or life/work redirections will not be achieved overnight.

At a gym, a good trainer begins by discussing the client's fitness goals. After clarifying her desired outcomes, the trainer may follow up by assessing the client's general health, heart rate, blood pressure, body fat, strength and flexibility. The trainer then spends time with the client designing a specific workout plan, with targets in a time frame that she commits to following.

A life/career coach will work with you in a similar fashion—using a variety of tools to support your life/career fitness, including asking you powerful questions, listening to your responses, reflecting with you on your challenges, helping you determine options and supporting your actions in moving toward your goals. In the same way that physical fitness requires you to get off the couch, build upon your strengths, exercise your options and keep active, life/career fitness also requires exercising your commitment to learning.

The following exercises can be helpful in beginning the life/career fitness process.

Exercise 1: Reflection and Assessment

Take some time to reflect on each of the questions below, then write your answers on a blank sheet of paper.

A. Purpose or Mission

Motivational speaker Zig Ziglar has noted that "outstanding people have one thing in common: an absolute sense of mission." Many of you desire to develop lives and careers that are meaningful and significant. You want assurance that you are making a difference in the world—living out the purpose or mission you were created to fulfill.

To help my clients tune in to their calling and purpose, we talk about the Source of their calling as well as the primary components that will help them understand their lives on a deeper level. If you have not done so before, ask yourself:

- What is my unique purpose?
- How is my life purpose reflected in my life roles?
- What do I hope to accomplish in my lifetime?
- What will a successful life and career look like?
- What would my personal mission statement say?

B. Passion

One of the primary clues to your purpose is reflected in those things that you are passionate about or energized when doing. Laurie Beth Jones, author of *The Path*, indicates that if you lack passion, you are on the wrong life/career path. Ask yourself:

- What gets me up in the morning?
- What can I do for hours on end without noticing the passage of time?
- What feedback have others given me about my enthusiasm for particular activities?
- If my current career does not stir my passion, what are the contributing factors as I see them?
- What would I like to change?

C. Particular Gifts and Talents

Each of you has a collection of talents and capacities, qualities, traits and spiritual gifts that uniquely distinguish you from every other person. Coaches can help you identify these gifts or prioritize the talents that you most enjoy using. If your work is a good match, it will be a natural expression of your talents. Thus, regardless of whether I am serving as a professor, consultant, course developer or team builder, I usually find myself using my gifts in a coaching role with my clients.

Just as a poorly-designed garment can be too tight, show signs of distress or pinch your skin, a poor career fit can likewise lead to emotional pinches, discontentment and stress. Ask yourself:

- What are my primary gifts and talents?
- What gifts and talents do I most enjoy using?
- What gifts and talents have I not used but would enhance my life/career?
- What attitudes are important to develop my strengths and address my weaknesses in a mature manner?

D. Principles or Values

Values clarification is often a component of career coaching. We all prize certain values and determine those which are non-negotiable in selecting our life/career directions. An ideal work environment reflects the values and personalities that are important to us.

Think about your preferences and values. You may prefer working alone or in teams, with high or low structure in your work designs, with great variety in activity or focused activity, in a high-action setting or with ample opportunity to think, with lots of freedom or with close supervision. Ask yourself:

- What values represent who I am?
- What are the three to five most important values to me in life and work?
- Where do my current life/work activities align well with my values?
- Where is there misalignment between my life/work and my values?

E. Place or Context

Career theorist John Holland has identified six primary environments that match personalities and interests of people with similar work settings. Clients can discover their preferences by taking assessment tools and discussing their findings with a career coach. Jane Kise, David Stark and Sandra Krebs Hirsch, authors of *Life Keys*, describe the type of people who are attracted to the six environments.

- **Realistic**: People who want to roll up their sleeves and get things done in practical ways
- **Investigative**: People who want to conduct research, sort through ideas and figure things out

- **Artistic**: People who are expressive and want to create something through writing, music or other outlets for their gifted imaginations
- **Social**: People who are people-oriented and collaborate to benefit others
- **Enterprising**: People who want to influence others and make things happen
- **Conventional**: People who provide structure and order to keep things running smoothly

In addition to these general preferences, clients can also favor environmentally-specific features such as natural lighting, open or closed office spaces, colorful or subdued decor and background music or solitude, to name a few. Ask yourself:

- What geographical location is important to me?
- What kind of organization will be a good match for me?
- What kinds of services or products are important to me?
- What kind of a work ecosystem is conducive to my productivity?
- How much freedom, activity, flexibility, people contact, travel, etc. make up an ideal work profile?

F. People

Not all coaches help clients focus on the types of people they want to work with. I have discovered, however, a great variance in such preferences. Some clients want to work with professional colleagues while others want to work with the poor. Some want to work with children, and others want to work only with adults.

Furthermore, clients vary in how they choose to work with people. They may want to influence, teach, sell to, counsel, entertain, provide products and services to, lead, protect, cure, feed or work with people in a variety of other ways. Clients who are not people-oriented may prefer to work with things or ideas rather than with people. Even in those cases, the product or service will benefit a particular customer group.

Using the Myers Briggs Type Indicator or another validated instrument, I help people discover their personality and/or behavioral preferences in greater detail so they will develop higher emotional intelligence (self-awareness, self-regulation and empathy for others) and increased understanding of the people with whom they want to work. Ask yourself:

- What groups or types of people do I want to have as customers or clients of my products or services?
- With what groups or types of people would I not work well?
- In what ways do I want to work with them?
- What style preferences do I have?
- How will I need to accommodate style differences in the way I work with people?

Exercise 2: Creating a Career Profile and Action Plan

You may take the first steps toward changing your future after you create and analyze a profile of your needs, desires and strengths from the data you have collected from your various assessments and coaching sessions.

The next step is to create an action plan in which you set both long- and short-term goals. Goals are intentions that must be translated into specific steps, with deadlines, so that your progress can be tracked. As you begin to work on your career goals, you may need to work through challenges or barriers, real or imagined, which can impede success. To avoid being derailed, you may need support in:

- Getting unstuck from old habits
- Working on blind spots in life/work
- Shunning a victim mentality
- Taking responsibility for their future
- Reducing perfectionist standards
- Eliminating drains from your life
- Dealing with burnout
- Surviving a layoff
- Determining your life after retirement
- Achieving better life/work balance, particularly in the use of leisure time
- Taking risks in new areas of interest
- Creating an updated resume
- Rehearsing successful interviewing techniques

I hope that these exercises are helpful to you in your quest for life and career fitness. Perhaps by taking hold of your future, you will capture the spirit and enthusiasm of playwright George Bernard Shaw, who said:

"I rejoice in life for its own sake. Life is no brief candle to me. It is a sort of splendid torch that I have got hold of for the moment, and I want to make it burn as brightly as possible before handing it on to future generations."

Selected Coaching References

Bandy, Thomas G.(2000). Coaching Change: Breaking Down Resistance, Building Up Hope. Abingdon Press.

Barlow, Cheri Allen. (1998) *Coaching Towards Excellence: Families & Groups*. Quest Center.

Collins, Gary (2001). *Christian Coaching*. Colorado Springs, Co. NavPress.

Crane, Thomas G. (1999). *The Heart of Coaching*. San Diego, Ca.: FTA Press.

Ellis, Dave. (1998). *Life Coaching: A New Career for Helping Professionals*. Breakthrough Enterprises.

Flaherty, James. (1999). *Coaching: Evoking Excellence in Others*. Boston, Ma: Butterworth-Heinemann.

Fortgang, Laura Berman (1998). *Take Yourself to the Top*. Warner Books.

Goldsmith, Marshall, Lyons, Laurence, and Freas, Alyssa. (2000). *Coaching for Leadership*. San Francisco, Ca: Jossey-Bass.

Gilley, Jerry. (1995) *Stop Managing, Start Coaching*! Irwin Publishing.

Hargrove. Robert. (2000). *The Masterful Coaching Fieldbook: Grow Your Business, Multiply Your Profits, Win the Talent War*. San Francisco, Ca.: Jossey-Bass.

Holliday, Micki. (2001). *Coaching, Mentoring, & Managing: A Coach Guidebook*. Franklin Lakes, N.J.: The Career Press, Inc.

Hudson, Frederic, (1997). *Personal and Organizational Coaching –a Profession for the Twenty-First Century*. Hudson Institute Press.

Hudson, Frederic. (1999). *The Handbook of Coaching*. San Francisco, Ca.: Jossey-Bass.

Hunt, James. M and Weintraub, Joseph R. (2002). *The Coaching Manager: Developing Top Talent in Business*. Thousand Oaks, Ca.: Sage Publications.

Leonard, Thomas J. (1998). *The Portable Coach: 28 Surefire Strategies for Business and Personal Success*. New York, NY: Scribner Press.

O'Neill, Mary Beth (2000), *Executive Coaching with Backbone and Heart: A Systems Approach to Engaging Leaders with Their Challenges.* Jossey-Bass.

Stanley, Paul D. and Clinton, J. Robert. (1992). *Connecting: The Mentoring Relationships You Need to Succeed in Life.* Colorado Springs, Co.: NavPress.

Whitworth, Laura, et. Al. (1998) *Co-Active Coaching: New Skills for Coaching People Toward Success in Work and Life.* Palo Alto, Ca.: Davies-Black.

Anita Schamber, Ed.D.

Dr. Anita Schamber, Certified Professional Coach, Counselor, and Speaker, wears two professional hats. First, she is a partner on a Global Learning Team which develops and coaches leaders globally for World Vision International, a Christian humanitarian organization. Second, as principal of Quality Life Associates, her coaching and training firm, Anita has served clients at AT&T, Boeing, IBM, hospitals, professional associations, universities, and churches. A "coach for all seasons," Anita's passion is to inspire, motivate, and equip clients to use God-given talents to fulfill their life/career purposes. Her results-focused strategies assist clients worldwide in bridging the gap from "good" to "abundant" living by focusing on spiritual foundations, life/career designs, balance, and leadership effectiveness. Anita is a frequent national conference speaker and an author of articles on coaching, which appear in *The Christian Management Report* and in an online newsletter, *"The Coach's Corner."* Anita has co-authored two books on effective learning and outstanding training programs on leadership and professional development, but she is best known for her personal investment in the success of others!

Dr. Anita L. Schamber
World Vision International
Global Learning Partners
"A Coach for All Seasons" [Ecc. 3:1]
(253) 815-2008, office
(253) 859-8948, home office

Office location:
World Vision US
P.O. Box 9716 MS248
Federal Way, WA 98063
aschambe@worldvision.org

Chapter 2

The Finesse Factor

Debbie Smith & Jill Mejia

This chapter contains influential skills you will need for achieving success. Society often dictates that getting a college degree is the "most" important step you can take; however, some employers disagree. Opportunities are often missed by the general population because they overlook or have never been taught "life-skills." Your fate can be decided, literally, in seconds. As unfair as that may seem, it's true. Our goal is to motivate and inspire you to exceed your potential by acquiring what we call "The Finesse Factor."

"What is The Finesse Factor?" you ask. The term encompasses a variety of behaviors and practices such as:

- How you enter a room and present yourself.
- How you shake hands and greet others.
- How attention to every detail about your appearance from head to toe is extremely important.

There are critics everywhere just waiting for the opportunity to pass judgment on you. Some employers or clients rule out candidates based on their appearance while others after the initial handshake. Gaining favorable endorsement can advance your career and unlock your potential, both personally and professionally. (An honest self-evaluation regarding one's liabilities can be unpleasant and difficult, however, is worth the time and investment.)

Although there are many schools of thought, the most successful insights we pass along come from years of research and experience, and, if utilized, will distinguish you from your competition. Does this mean you will go straight to the top? Not necessarily. However, image and social savvy are contributing factors when it comes to promotability or sealing the deal. "Finesse" requires the desire to be your very best. Those who say, "I haven't needed it so far," may be sabotaging their career. Your colleagues may at first overlook your blunders, but they won't for long. You may be passed over in favor of those who continually practice and stay up with the times. A polished image and good manners are not optional; they are the essential skills you need to succeed.

The harsh reality is that we live in a remote-control society and our attention spans are shorter than ever. It takes no more than a glance to form an impression, which doesn't give you much time to prove yourself. Employers are willing to pay more if you already look the part. They begin to evaluate you, based on their visual perception, and upon which they then form irreversible judgments. This can even happen while you're walking away, so never leave any fine detail to chance. The bad news is that most people do not want to analyze their own liabilities. The good news is that your visual impact is the easiest one to alter yet many people resist the most.

We believe that during your initial encounter with others, your visual impact and attitude equal ninety-three percent of their first impression and that only seven percent is attributed to your words, tone of voice and personality. Experts agree that social savvy is not something you know instinctively; it requires training and consulting. We have found that sixty percent of first impressions are accurate. It's time to roll up your sleeves and put an action plan together with practical information that will create immediate results.

Employers and clients form their initial impressions based on:

- The quality of your clothing, style, the accessories you wear and your personal grooming.
- Posture, how you carry yourself and the quality of your handshake.
- Non-verbal communication and how you respond to others.
- Dining, business and social savvy.
- Presenting business cards and networking skills.
- Tattoos and body piercings.
- The type of car you drive.

During those first few moments they make assumptions regarding:

- Education and economic level
- Sophistication and social position
- Self-confidence and attitude
- Personality
- Current mood

It never ceases to amaze us how many people overlook the importance of "life-skills." We truly believe they communicate credibility, leadership and confidence. These powerful attributes then give you the chance to prove yourself. The sad side to this is that our future leaders are not being taught this valuable information, which puts them at a huge competitive disadvantage in our society.

Polish Your Brass!

Years ago, when the general public was allowed on-board visitation of naval vessels, my dad treated our family to an outing on an aircraft carrier. We proceeded to the bridge, where I remember being amazed at how everything gleamed like gold.

I asked, "Dad, is this gold?"

He smiled and said, "No, Baby Doll, it's brass."

"What do they have to do to make it look like that?" I asked.

"They have to polish it every day, because the minute you stop polishing brass, it begins to tarnish." Years later, I realized the point of that answer. We should all polish our soft-skills every day, so we, too, can gleam like gold.

Seven Critical Questions We Need To Ask Ourselves

1. What does my image convey?
2. Am I raising doubts with those I meet?
3. Do I execute an impressive handshake?
4. How are my networking skills?
5. Do I know when and how to give out a business card with finesse?
6. Am I a solution finder or a whiner?
7. Do I possess a positive attitude?

Question: Are you ready to take action and really see what others see? We believe reinventing yourself takes courage and commitment in order to pursue your dreams. We certainly aren't here to instill fear, however, the reality is that the competition in the job market is at an all-time high, and in order to keep people intrigued, you must give them a reason.

Ignoring the Importance of Your Visual Impact Can Have Serious Consequences!

Wayne was a self-employed computer repairman. One day, he was giving a presentation at a networking meeting in a wrinkled shirt, no tie, stained pants and scuffed shoes. He had been in business for years and always seemed to be struggling. We spoke after the meeting, and we discussed his effectiveness. This reality test shocked him, and at that very moment, he decided to hire our consulting firm. After a few minor adjustments, we attended the same meeting the next week. As soon as he walked through the door, several people came up to Wayne and asked him for his card saying, "Wow, do you look great!"

Wayne had more business than ever and was enjoying the attention. The story, however, takes a downturn. He returned to his old ways of not making an effort to work on his image presentation, and his business resumed its spiral downward. He felt it was too much trouble to keep up with the attempt to make a difference. The "take me as I am" attitude is risky when you want to advance in business or society.

Embarrassing Moment!

Has there ever been a time you just wanted to crawl into a hole because of the way you were dressed? Especially when it related to your business? Don't you wish you could take it back and do it over? This happened to me! Oh, yes! Forgetting that I had listed my occupation as an Image Consultant on the patient information sheet, I rushed my son to our new dentist's office dressed in my worst workout clothes. My hair was in a pony tail, and I had on absolutely no make-up -- a very scary sight for those not used to seeing me that way! "It's just a quick visit," I reasoned, "and then I'll do that workout." The dentist walked in with his clipboard, studied the information, paused to look me up and down and asked, "So, how long have you been an Image Consultant?" I wanted to die on the spot! I didn't know doctors read the patient's information. I've been "dressed to the nines" ever since. But, it doesn't matter now.

The first impression I made was a lasting one, and I doubt I will ever be hired for consulting at that office. What a lesson I had to learn the hard way!

Who's In Charge?

Think about a time when you saw a man and a woman standing next to each other, both in professional attire. Who would you say was in charge? Ninety percent will always say that it is the man. Sorry ladies, that's still the real world we live in. Truth is, however, that if the gentleman took off his jacket, you would then agree that the woman was in charge. The next time you're out and about, observe this incredible example and see for yourself that a lot of your visual credibility is in the coat you wear, if you want to be taken seriously.

Let The Sales Soar!

One day, during a presentation at a Chamber of Commerce meeting, a young man stood up and gave a testimonial. He used to work for a company that allowed its employees to wear Hawaiian shirts (that was their dress code). The company's representatives had relied on trade shows for the bulk of their business, but when new management came on board, they decided that their casual image was not appropriate. They made it mandatory to go back to a more conservative look. You guessed it -- suits. This mandate took a struggling company to a very profitable organization. Its sales began to soar after a few minor adjustments. We should never underestimate how others see our outer packaging. This goes for any company that wants to make a positive impression. In addition, your front-line also represents the company image. It would be a crucial mistake to think it doesn't matter.

Professional Packaging

Even before you speak a word, the quality of your appearance and clothing speaks volumes. You must be attentive to every detail. Assumptions about you and your business are made within seconds, and sometimes it only has to do with your appearance and manners. This can be a benefit or a detriment. Eighty percent of anyone's perception is based on non-verbal signs and it's up to you to control the message you are sending.

When building a wardrobe, we recommend that you purchase complete basic outfits you can mix and match. This should include conservative styles, of the best quality you can afford. Cheap handbags, shoes, briefcases, purses, ties, acrylic scarves and plastic jewelry will diminish your successful image as well. Select neutral colors such as navy, gray, burgundy and black.

The color navy is the most approachable where black can be very intimidating.

Men's Essentials:
1. Four or five suits
2. Five shirts
3. Five ties

Women's Essentials:
1. Four suits (look for three-piece or four-piece suits)
2. Five blouses
3. Two skirts
4. Two pants
5. Two scarves

This represents forty different outfits, one for every day for two months. Remember, the secret here is that all your colors and textures must work well together. Your blouses and accessories, shirts and ties are where you showcase your personality and flair. However, don't get silly or frilly.

The Power of Color

This is the first thing someone notices. Certain colors can make you look fabulous while others can make you appear pale and lifeless. We suggest that both men and women save themselves time and money by making an appointment to have their colors analyzed by a professional consultant. All of us have our own unique skin tones, eye color and hair color. As you discover the right palette for you, you will see that they have more impact than you could ever imagine! Why do you always reach for that certain item in your closet? The answer – color!

There is nothing finer than a crisp white shirt or blouse to polish up a business suit, right? Are we recommending the standard bright white for everyone, as if "one shade fits all?" Not really, because not all whites are created equal: icy white, soft white, cream and ivory are just a few of our choices. For some, a winter white will make them look stunning; for others, that shade will drain them of color and bring out all their shadows and imperfections. Men will appear as if they need to shave again, and women will have to apply more makeup to look flawless.

So how can you learn which is your best white? Here's an exercise you can do to move closer to the right one. Under natural lighting, stand in front of a mirror, place each of the shades of white under your chin and study your face. Do you see lines, shadows and flaws? Does one of the shades drain you of color? Or, do you look younger, well-rested and have more natural color? Do you notice your eyes first? Or, are you drawn to the imperfections? Remember, it's all about making the most of your personal palette of color, and your optimum shade of white will help you look your absolute best!

Why It Can Be Life-Changing!

Do you have that thousand-dollar makeup drawer? I did! Years ago, when the concept first became popular, I had my "colors" analyzed. Unfortunately, there were only four seasons to choose from, and the consultant told me that I was a "winter." After turning forty, I found it harder and harder to find the right makeup and clothing colors. It was frightening! I'd check my makeup in all different lighting—even carrying a little mirror into a grocery store to see what I looked like under fluorescent lights. You should have seen the strange looks I got from the people in the store! Nothing looked right, and I could not figure out why. I finally made a decision to have my "colors" done in the updated 12-palette system. I'll never forget the reaction when I came home.

My husband said, "Honey, you look fifteen years younger!"

And my eight year-old son squealed, "Mommy! You finally match!" Now that's approval! It was not just a life-changing experience for me-- it launched a new career.

Another question: When you select your clothing, do you know what styles look best on you, or do you go into the dressing room and come out frustrated? Would you like to know a secret or two that can help with that dilemma? Of course you would. Another question that will pique your interest: When you look in your closet, do you wear just ten percent of what is in there? Most people would have to answer, "Yes!" Why? Because we know it is going to fit just right, and you get the most compliments when wearing that item.

(For tips on how to re-organize your closet which saves you time and money, contact us through our web site at www.finessefactor.com.)

ILLUSION DRESSING

Evaluate Your Liabilities:

- Clothing with horizontal lines adds ten to twenty pounds to your appearance.
- Double-breasted suits can make you look heavier (single-breasted suits with one row of buttons create the illusion of being thinner).

- Wearing two separate colors, such as a white shirt or blouse with black pants, also creates an objectionable horizontal line.
- Anywhere you do not want to accentuate a liability, do not allow a hemline, belt or color to draw one's eyes to that area.

Enhance Your Assets:

- Vertical lines add height and are more visually slimming.
- A row of vertical buttons draws one's eyes up and down (ladies, this also applies to jewelry, such as longer necklaces).
- Wearing all one color elongates the visual effect.
- Diagonal lines are the most flattering for women.
- Ladies, a pin or broach brings attention to your eyes and is a great conversation piece. Gold is the preferred color for jewelry in the professional world.

INVESTMENT DRESSING

Buy quality clothing the first time -- it lasts longer and it is worth the investment. Here's a formula that will help you decide for yourself. Let's say you're considering buying a classic-style blazer -- a timeless piece. Let's do the math: If the item costs $175.00 divided by 108 wearings (3 times a month for the next 3 years) equals $1.62 each time you wear it. Add on the cleaning bill of $1.50 per month (only fifty cents per wearing), and this item will cost you only $2.12 every time you put it on. This is less than the cost of a Latte! Now that would be a good investment, don't you agree? Try using this formula every time you decide to buy an item of clothing, and see if it is worth buying a trendy piece that will only be worn once in awhile.

Attention To Fine Details

The condition of your shoes and fingernails (whether you're a man or women) plays a critical role in the perception of your way of doing business. People observe these details when you're coming and going, signing contracts and shaking hands.

Worn-Out Shoes!

Have you ever worn down those little rubber tips on your heels and continued to walk around on the nails? I have been guilty of this one. Once while employed at a very busy bank, I was in a hurry coming back from lunch. The nails at the bottom of my heels caused me to go skidding across the tile floor. With nothing to stop me from falling flat on my face in a rather short skirt, I grabbed one poor gentleman by his ears. He was no taller than my shoulders, and when I pulled his face into my chest to regain my balance, the entire teller line started applauding. As the gentleman backed away, he said, "Oh, thank you, thank you, thank you." Just to let you know, this was the last time I ever let my shoes get that bad. Always keep your shoes in top condition by utilizing your local shoe repairman.

HOW TO LOSE CREDIBILITY IN A CONSERVATIVE BUSINESS

Women lose credibility when they:
1. Wear anything too loose, tight, low, sexy, sheer or sleeveless.
2. Are showing undergarments, bare legs or runs in their nylons.
3. Fail to cover all tattoos or remove all body piercings.
4. Chew gum or use a toothpick in public.
5. Wear scuffed or worn out shoes.
6. Wear too much perfume or over-accessorize. Jewelry should be simple but elegant.
7. Wear too much or too little makeup.

Tips For Women:
- It is a proven fact that wearing a natural application of makeup will improve your opportunities. Never underestimate this important secret.
- Bare legs send the wrong message in a professional environment.
- Closed-toed shoes are the standard in corporate attire.
- Coloring your hair may be an option, but keep it consistent with your skin tone as you mature.
- A quality briefcase, leather notepad and an elegant writing instrument broadcasts a professional image and pays big dividends for your career.
- Not accepting compliments or giving them is usually a sign of low self-confidence.

Men lose credibility when they:
1. Wear hats and sunglasses indoors.
2. Wear short sleeves.
3. Wear ties that are silly or are of improper length.
4. Wear poor quality suits.
5. Wear socks that don't cover the calf.
6. Wear scuffed or worn-out shoes.
7. Fail to cover all tattoos or remove all body piercings.
8. Chew gum or use a toothpick in public.
9. Wear too much cologne or jewelry.

Tips For Men:
- Facial hair and longer hair length may not be acceptable in a conservative professional environment.
- Coloring your hair may be an option, but it could actually make you look older past a certain age.
- A quality briefcase, leather notepad and an elegant writing instrument broadcasts a professional image and can pay big dividends for your career.
- Not accepting compliments or giving them is usually a sign of low self-confidence.

Body Piercings and Tattoos -- A Very Sensitive Subject!

These topics are probably the most sensitive subjects among our youth today and are ones against which we receive the most resistance. I was teaching a workshop when I met Nadia, a girl with a tongue piercing. She was not only beautiful, but extremely bright and talented. I felt compelled to ask, "Were you hired with that tongue piercing?"

"Funny you should ask," she replied. "Actually, there were four of us who applied. Three of us took out our piercings. All of us got hired except the person who left hers in."

I said, "That's interesting. What made you do that?"

"I thought it would give me the competitive edge," she said.

I replied, "Why did you put it back in?"

She responded, "I want to be a trailblazer."

"Do you realize," I told her, "that by wearing that piercing, you have now created a sensitive issue that your employer has to deal with? In addition, this action could even sabotage your career! One more thought to consider, Nadia -- trailblazers never reap the rewards of their actions; it's those behind them who usually enjoy the benefits."

She said, "I never thought of it that way. Thank you for bringing that to my attention." Since that day, she has never worn the piercing again and is now being recognized as a leader.

I Don't Understand—I'm So Qualified!

Dressing appropriately for job interviews is crucial to your career. One young lady came up to us after we spoke at the L.A. Job Fair. She was fluffing and playing with her beautiful, long, blond hair while she was telling us that she did not get a pharmaceutical sales position.

"I just don't understand why I wasn't hired! I am so qualified!" she explained. We were distracted by the way she constantly played with her hair. Then we noticed her short skirt, tanned bare legs and her low-cut neckline. Talk about a beauty! She told us she'd had a female interviewer, and we instantly understood why she hadn't been hired. Some females feel threatened or do not want a provocative image representing their organization. So she disqualified herself by her overall appearance.

Too-Sexy Apparel!

Dressing too sexy for male interviewers can be a problem as well. When I was in my early twenties (and naïve), I wore a tight, short skirt and a low-cut blouse when applying for a banking job. They hired me within minutes, even though there weren't any positions available at the time. They just put me in a chair until they could figure it out! Although I was flattered on one hand, they never took me seriously the entire time I was employed by them. No matter how hard I tried to prove myself, that first sexy impression was a lasting one—and a detriment to the start of my career.

Does Your Image Include Your Car?

In our opinion, at least in Southern California, image definitely includes your car. Just as you might have second thoughts regarding the sales capability of a real estate agent when he/she drives up in a beat-up, exhaust-belching car, the same holds true for every professional.

One day, I was starting a series of etiquette classes for a private school. I had been in a rush and didn't find the time to have my car washed. And it was dirty, believe me. So, I gave it some thought. I hadn't met any of the parents, or any of the teachers, for that matter. Should I show up early all dressed up and hope they overlook my car? After all, I'll just dazzle them with my presentation. Or should I get my car cleaned and present the total polished image? I chose the latter, and I must tell you, it was worth the extra effort. I observed the nods of approval from the parents and staff. I received their favorable endorsement right upfront, which made my credibility soar because it was consistent from start to finish. Yes, our vehicles can be a reflection of our professional image.

Image and Interviews!

At one time, I was a recruiter for a major airline. We sent out letters to applicants, requesting that they wear business attire. Those who ignored that request were not granted an interview. This really upset some applicants because they may have walked there, taken the bus or requested time off from work. Getting into the airlines was extremely competitive, and if applicants failed to follow instructions upfront, we believed that such applicants could become problematic later on in their careers. This criterion was also applied to those who were late, and to those who had a questionable attitude. We never hired out of desperation, and there was always a waiting list to even get an interview. Being one's very best was the standard back then, and this still rings true today.

The Client Thinks I'm In Charge!

One of my good friends found herself changing careers in the middle of her life. After years of being a preschool teacher, she went back to school and got her license as a real estate agent. Knowing that her wardrobe would have to shift from child-friendly denim to professional suits, she paid me a visit for a color, makeup and wardrobe consultation. We wanted to position her as a future top producer, and the results were phenomenal. Looking younger and feeling more professional, she took her "color wallet" and wardrobe suggestions with her on an exciting shopping expedition. Just one month into her new career, she exclaimed, "The clients think I'm in charge! They come into the office asking me questions as if I'm the manager! Even my boss has noticed how professional I look on a daily basis." As her clientele builds and sales climb, she exudes a new level of confidence in herself!

Social Savvy

Pretend for a moment that you were the owner or president of your own company and that you had to decide who to hire. Would you hire someone who was rough around the edges, or a person that would represent your company with a polished manner and a positive attitude? Of course, you'd recruit "the cream of the crop."

This is where social savvy gives you the chance to prove yourself. A firm handshake communicates a powerful message of confidence and credibility in business skills. Hold eye contact until you can tell the color of the other person's eyes. A pleasant smile will show that you're interested, and it will also set the tone for the conversation. When executing a confident handshake, use your right hand, connect web- to-web with firm pressure (not bone-crushing), shake vertically for two pumps, then release. Avoid clasping with the fingertips, shaking excessively or rotating the hands to where one is on top of the other. The other person will never take you seriously, and they may even be offended. If you are meeting international guests, you may want to brush up on appropriate greetings through books or training on global etiquette.

Dining Savvy

According to statistics, more than half of all business meetings and interviews are now being conducted at the dining table. People make character judgments based on: how you handle yourself, poise, courtesy, gestures, body language, what you order, how you order, use your utensils, where you sit and table conversation. Employers understand how these time-honored methods play a vital role in their company's success. Therefore, knowing these refinements make dining more enjoyable and can give you the competitive edge.

Things To Remember While Dining

1. The most important guest is seated to the host's right, and the second most honored guest is to the host's left.
2. The host should be seated facing away from the wall so that he can summon the server easily.
3. Turn off cell phones and pagers, or at least silence them. Do not carry on a phone conversation inside a restaurant or public facility.
4. Ask for menu recommendations when you are unsure of what to order. This way, you get an idea of what you should spend.
5. When meeting with CEOs or dignitaries, Continental or European style dining is the standard in formal protocol. Using Continental style, the knife and fork remain in the right and left hands, respectively, throughout the meal. The fork tines are always turned downward.

6. It is your responsibility to pass the food in front of you to the right.

7. The server will serve from the left and remove from the right.

8. Butter plates go on the left, and drinks go on the right.

9. When you begin to use your utensils, work from the outside inward.

10. Don't hang items on your chair if there is a chance they might fall on the floor.

11. Don't place your keys, briefcase, purse, cell phone or sunglasses on the table.

12. Dress appropriately. If you are unsure, phone the host in advance. Gentlemen, keep your coats on unless local culture/host dictates otherwise.

13. Don't rest your elbows on the table.

14. Avoid food that is awkward to eat (i.e. French onion soup, ribs, shellfish and spaghetti).

15. Don't overeat or drink too much. It appears low class.

16. Place the napkin on your lap after the order for drinks has been taken. Use it often.

17. It is impolite to salt your food before you taste it.

18. When having soup, fill the spoon by moving it away from you. Don't blow on the soup to cool it down. When most of the soup is finished, you may tip the bowl away from you to spoon out the last bit.

19. Never cut your food into many small pieces before you start to eat. Cut only one bite at a time.

20. Do only one thing at a time—either eat or drink. This causes food particles to float and swirl inside the glass from backwash.

21. Remember to swallow before speaking. Keep pace with others at the table.

22. Bread or rolls should be broken into bite-size pieces, and then only the piece you are going to eat should be buttered.

23. Do not burp, yawn, or use your napkin as a handkerchief. Cover your mouth when coughing.

24. Never interrupt the conversation or finish others' sentences.

25. Never use profanity or tell inappropriate jokes.

26. Ladies, don't apply lipstick at the table. Indiscreetly licking your lips will keep lipstick from sticking to the rim of the glass.

27. When leaving the table for any reason, place your napkin on your chair, push in your chair and say, "Please excuse me for a moment." Be brief. Or you can leave the napkin on the left side of the plate. Don't be surprised if the server brings you a fresh napkin.

28. Never get caught taking medication in front of client, especially if it is for an upset stomach, headache or heart medication. The client/interviewer may question your health condition.

29. When you are finished, place your knife and fork parallel to each other with the blade of the knife facing the fork. The prongs may be up or down. Leave your napkin to the right of your plate.

30. When you invite someone for a meal, you pay!

31. For a touch of class, write a thank-you note to the host.

The good news is that you can learn good table manners in a couple of hours, which includes taking several opportunities to practice. Never assume that others will not notice bad manners; you must be sensitive to what others see! Your behavior and appearance, good or bad, can open or close the doors to your success. (Tip: practice in front of a mirror.)

Things To Remember About Business Etiquette

1. Return phone calls and e-mails promptly.

2. If you must cancel appointments, call personally, apologize and suggest to reschedule.

3. On formal or informal invitations, you may see the acronym R.S.V.P. It means that you should let the person who invited you know whether or not you are attending within 48 hours of receiving the invitation. Never assume the other person knows you're coming. You may find out you're not on the list and be refused at the door. Also, the event planner needs this information to order what's needed.

4. Don't put your personal items such as a briefcase, glasses, keys, sunglasses or any other item on the person's desk, and don't touch anything on his/her desk unless invited to do so.

5. Avoid asking the receptionist to use her phone.

6. Avoid eating or multitasking while on the phone. Give the other person your full attention.

7. Never shake hands across the desk. Walk around and greet your client or guest.
8. When invited to a party, always take a small, non-personal gift.
9. Stand when being introduced. Those that don't will sink in the estimation of others.
10. Stand when a visitor or a lady enters the room.
11. Never take personal phone calls during a meeting.
12. If you have to leave a meeting early, be sure to tell the host before the meeting begins.
13. Never use someone's first name without permission to do so.

Networking Savvy

1. Determine who you want to meet and what you want to accomplish at the event.
2. Prepare seven-second introductions for different events.
3. Purchase a professional name tag and wear it on the right shoulder.
4. Don't monopolize anyone's time.
5. Share resources and ask questions (but nothing personal).
6. Get involved in committees.
7. Make others feel comfortable.
8. Have a business card even if you are unemployed. It is vital to your professional success, and adds a touch of class to your personal life. Never hand out one that is worn, smudged or has information that is incorrect or crossed out. Be selective when giving out your card until there is a request, otherwise, you will appear overeager.
9. Hold your beverage in your left hand so your right hand is free and dry in order to shake hands.
10. Learn global etiquette.
11. Follow up immediately on any requests.
12. Never ask for a contact at an event. Wait until a couple days later.
13. Don't promise what you can't deliver.
14. Avoid ethnic or gender jokes, sarcasm and gossip.
15. Stay away from controversial issues.

Turn Off That Cell Phone!

The latest social faux pas is the use of cell phones in certain public places. Not only is it rude to make others overhear your conversation, but it can complicate matters in everyday life. Picture this: I was in the middle of a busy salad bar line, when I was forced to listen to a conversation a beautiful young lady was having on her cell phone. She had the phone cradled against her neck while she was building her salad. Apparently, whatever she heard was too much to bear, because her phone suddenly slipped from her neck and fell into the tub of ranch dressing – right in front of all of us! Dressing, anyone?

Thank-You Notes Reap Many Benefits

If you really want to stand above the crowd, request the interviewer's business card (for correct title and spelling) and handwrite a thank-you note within forty-eight hours of an encounter. This gesture never goes unnoticed—especially after a job interview. Most employers agree that when they receive a thank-you note it leaves a lasting impression of class. Even though you may not get the job during that hiring session, they may consider you first for future openings.

Quick Reference of the Top Thirteen Credibility Boosters

1. A professional appearance opens doors. Update your look periodically.
2. Social savvy helps position you for greater opportunities.
3. Don't remove your coat. It can discount your credibility.
4. The condition of your shoes and fingernails tells others if you are detailed-oriented.
5. Cover tattoos and remove body piercings. Be conservative.
6. Body language speaks volumes, even when you're silent.
7. Know the value of an impressive handshake.
8. Know when to give out a business card.
9. Be on time to every engagement and appointment.
10. Return all phone calls and e-mails promptly.
11. Never leave your cell phone or pager on in a public building. Set it on vibrate.
12. Learn global etiquette so you won't be caught off guard and offend someone.
13. Send thank-you notes. It's worth the effort.

In closing, we know you are under tremendous pressure to do more with less time, and your survival depends upon your knowledge and practice of these time-honored methods. It is a proven fact that people gravitate towards those who utilize good manners and have a polished image. They tend to receive more referrals. Our challenge to you now is to begin investing in your future and never underestimate the power of your "Finesse Factor." The perceptions of those who hold your future in their hands are the only ones that count! By mastering these concepts, we guarantee it will be useful to you throughout your career and personal relationships. These skills can, and should, last a lifetime!

Debbie Smith & Jill Mejia

Debbie Smith and Jill Mejia are professional speakers, authors and certified professional image and social savvy consultants. They specialize in working with college students, individuals, associations and private industry to enhance and polish their professional development. They have over twenty-five years combined related experience in public speaking, training, recruiting, management, customer service and women's special interests. They are represented in the American Society of Training and Development, Healthcare Speakers Bureau and the National Speakers Association. They were featured keynote speakers for the Los Angeles Times Career Fair. They have received outstanding reviews for fast and easy reality-based training seminars and are well-known for their professional platform skills, passionate delivery style and entertaining presentations that get results!

The Finesse Factor

Debbie Smith, (562) 943-8718
Email: Debbie@FinesseFactor.com

Jill Mejia, (714) 528-6941
Email: Jill@FinesseFactor.com

Website: www.FinesseFactor.com

Chapter 3

The Downsizing Survival Guide

Ted Janusz

Downsizing—it doesn't always make a lot of sense. It's like a basketball coach calling a time out, huddling with her team and saying, "We're way behind in this game, so this calls for some drastic measures. Chelsea, Heidi—you're on the bench. We're going to win this game with just three players!"

Has anything like this happened to you in your work lately? If so, it has probably left you wondering whatever happened to the notion of, "Employees are our most important assets." If you have, indeed, been downsized, rightsized, de-hired, reengineered or whatever euphemism you would like to use for "out of a job," I'm here to tell you that you can still survive, and even thrive, as a result.

About a quarter to nine one morning, my boss stopped at my desk. "Patrick needs to see us at nine," he nonchalantly informed me, referring to his boss. As I passed through Patrick's door an hour later, my boss motioned me to sit down, then began, "We've decided to let you go." After those opening words, I can't really remember what else he had to say. Suddenly, it seemed as though my spirit had left my body to hover near the ceiling. I was participating in the event in the third person. "You'll have until ten-thirty to gather up all of your belongings," I was told.

That was it? After three-and-a-half years of service, that was the farewell I got? No time to tie up loose ends or say goodbye to friends? Didn't I deserve at least a bit more?

That was the third—and thus far, the last—layoff of my career. Of the three separation experiences, it was definitely the most painful. But allow me to go back and start at the beginning.

The First Layoff

My first layoff ended my initial job out of graduate school. Before my graduation in 1979, I had received two job offers—one from a Midwestern computer hardware manufacturer for $18,000 and one from a management consulting firm headquartered near Washington, D.C., for $23,000.

When I arrived at the computer manufacturer for the interview, I was under the impression that I was trying out for a position in international marketing. Instead, they told me they had just undergone a reorganization (obviously a bad omen) and that the position was no longer available. "But would you like to interview for an opening in our finance department?" I was asked. I thought, "Why not?"

Shortly, I was introduced to a gentleman whose warmth and personality could have made a slug look like the life of the party. As he launched into a tirade of buzzwords, I suddenly had the mental image of toiling beneath this boorish boss for the next twenty or thirty years.

Instead, I chose what I thought was the higher paying position, the one with the management consulting firm. I knew that the company would soon recognize my many talents and find a position suitable for a newly minted MBA like myself. The new decade of the '80s started off badly, however, when the home office told me I had been laid off. Pink slip number one. The recession of the time had caused the loss of a number of government contracts for the firm, and I was one of the resulting casualties.

In retrospect, had I taken the job with the Midwestern computer manufacturer, I could have availed myself of myriad internal training programs offered by the company. I would only have to have served under Mr. Personality for six months to a year, and then, using my newfound skills, moved on to a position more to my liking. Instead, I hastily chose the management consulting firm, which lacked such infrastructure and whose objective was to farm out associates as quickly as possible to get billable hours, often in faraway locations and with little or no preparation.

In all fairness to myself, how was a new graduate expected to know this? All that I had known since kindergarten was how to go to school. Sure, I had mastered that process. But at graduation, it was as though I had suddenly been exploded out of a tunnel. The possibilities seemed endless. How could I know what I should do unless I fell and bloodied myself a few times? Hindsight can be, but is not always, twenty-twenty.

"Show me someone who knows what they want to do with the rest of their life at age seventeen," says Barbara Moses, Ph.D. and author of *Creating Your Authentic Career*, "and I'll show you someone who will be going through a mid-life career crisis at age thirty-five."

Moral: Don't go directly to graduate school. Enter the real world first. Make a few mistakes there. Then return to your safe haven, where your slate can be wiped clean by an intermediate term of schooling before you seek the right job.

The Second Layoff

Within a year, I would again be the victim of a layoff—this time, at my very next job. The telecommunications company that had purchased the computer timesharing firm I was working for decided to consolidate the marketing operations in their headquarters in Kansas City. I was not asked to make the move. Although I was immediately reassigned a position (averting the possible disaster of a lengthy layoff), I soon left the company on my own. The continual series of reorganizations rocked the company and left the operations in a shambles.

Moral: Beware of going to work for any company that has been newly purchased or merged.

What could I have done instead? After my third layoff, I realized that there were many things I could have done to avoid the pitfalls of downsizing and enhance my career potential at the same time. The good news is that you, too, can take advantage of these strategies, whether you are currently employed or have recently been the victim of corporate shrinkage.

IF YOU ARE CURRENTLY EMPLOYED

Develop an Attitude of "Me, Inc."

As the sole owner and sole employee of Me, Inc., your only job throughout your career is to develop and market a single product – you.

According to the Bureau of Labor Statistics, "Me, Inc." is going to face 10.3 job changes over the course of a working life. Employment experts predict that the average worker will also undergo five career changes. Remember that as secure as you might feel now, nothing lasts forever.

What appeals to a person at age twenty-five may not look as attractive at thirty-five. Most of us like to learn and grow, and you may eventually find that you would like to grow in another area. As a result, you will be more effective over the course of your career if you think of yourself as "Me, Inc.," your own "personal services" company.

Provide Value

If you are currently employed, calculate how much you are being paid today. Add in any additional benefits like health care coverage, vacation pay or company 401(k) benefits.

Now think about what you did today to earn that money. Sure, we all have unproductive days, but do you believe (in a slight twist on Woody Allen's famous observation) that eighty percent of your pay should be based on just showing up? Have you or others at work adopted the attitude that your company should consider itself lucky just to have you around? Danielle Kennedy refers to these people as "the quicksand crowd." The Gallup Organization knows them as the "ROAD (Retired On Active Duty) warriors."

Instead, "dollarize" your contributions. Think: "What did I do today to add to my company's bottom line, in excess of what I was paid? (In the long run, it is the only reason you job even exists.) Also think: "What can I do to increase my value to make sure that I stay continually 'in the black?'"

To put this in perspective, let's say that you owned your company and were faced with the prospect of hiring salespeople. Each salesperson costs you $100 per day but will close $110 worth of business each day. How many would you hire? Theoretically, as many as you could find!

On the other hand, let's assume each salesperson still costs you $100 per day, has a great attitude and is dedicated, friendly and dressed to kill. But what if each can only manage to bring in $90 per day? Now how many would your hire? None! In this case, you would lose $10 per day on each additional hire.

Moral: Be like the $110-per-day salesperson.

Reinvent Yourself

The most successful companies compete against themselves, primarily so that nobody else will. Hewlett-Packard comes out with a less expensive model of printer with more features. Intel introduces a more powerful computer processor.

What about you? Could a younger, cheaper worker easily replace you? Or could you even be displaced by technology? Intel co-founder and chairman, Andy Grove, has a motto that has contributed to his continual success: "Only the paranoid survive."

On the other hand, consider Lou, the old-timer we once had on our work force. Everybody loved Lou, and Lou loved everybody. Whether a seminar was being given on campus or a birthday was being celebrated, you could always count on Lou to be there—unless he was napping at his desk. Management knew that Lou only had a few years to go until retirement, so they graciously left him alone. But when new management took over, they asked, "Who is this?" Lou is now gone.

Moral: Don't be a Lou.

Executive recruiter Charles Grevious says, "The truth of the matter is, job security is a thing of the past. The only thing you can do now is work on employability security—building the right skills and learning to market yourself aggressively."

Promote Yourself Internally

In the last round of layoffs at my company, management admitted they had let some of the wrong people go. These people had done nothing but silently perform the jobs they were expected to do. Management didn't realize how valuable some of these people were until they were gone. These people had toiled under the mistaken belief that if they just worked hard and kept to themselves, everything would be okay.

And after three downsizing experiences of my own, you can probably understand why I, still, am a little paranoid. As a result, I try to make at least one professional and one personal contact each day.

You may be a humble person. And humility is a desirable trait on the job. You may say, "I could never be comfortable blowing my own horn." That's fine. After all, nobody likes a blustery braggart who spends his or her time pointing out personal accomplishments to everyone. But that doesn't preclude you from promoting yourself.

One of the ways you can do so is by offering to help. For instance, I wanted to be a speaker at our company's annual customer conference. I sent an e-mail to one of the organizers to tell her that I could be available at a moment's notice in the case of a cancellation and that I had already spoken on the same topic at another conference. In other words, I answered the question, "What's in it for her?" (More on that later.) Then, and only then, did I list my qualifications for her. I got the speaking engagement.

Another suggestion is to do quality work. Then volunteer to serve on cross-functional teams within your company. Think of these steps as on-the-job insurance.

Moral: By ignoring it, office politics will not simply go away. Learn how to make office politics work for you, rather than against you.

Promote Yourself Externally

The reference section of your library is likely to have the *Encyclopedia of Associations* on its shelf. The book lists more than 17,000 associations that could be of interest to you. Joining such groups can give you valuable knowledge, but the friendships, support and contacts you can make may prove to be invaluable.

Meet others who have similar interests and positions in other companies. These contacts could prove to be helpful should you ever need to look for a position beyond your current employer.

Become a Mentor

Get into situations where others "owe you" in a career sense. But don't collect. Take someone new to your field, show him or her the ropes and let him or her benefit from your experience. These people will remember you and can be there when you really need their help further down the line. George H. Bush used this "Rolodex diplomacy" to help propel himself into the White House.

Don't Burn Bridges

My third downsizing experience had a happy ending. Fourteen months afterward, I was asked to come back to the company by the vice president who had been in the room when I was dismissed. Had our dealings during or after my departure been stormy, I would have never been given a second chance.

You probably work with some whiners and complainers at your office. Most work-related problems are people issues rather than knowledge or competence issues, but because of the legal implications of a termination, companies are hesitant to fire even the malcontents. At the time of a mass layoff, however, it's relatively easy for management to make sure that the bad apples are a key ingredient in the departing applesauce.

Maintain Key Information

To protect themselves after announcing a layoff, companies usually require all affected employees to depart immediately. In my case, my only copy of my resume was on my computer's hard drive. But I was fortunate. My boss allowed me to return to the office after hours to retrieve it.

Work for the Person Who Hired You

I was once hired to work in an all-female office. Heaven on earth? No, it was quite the opposite. The vice president in Boston (a male) made the decision to hire me, but my boss in Pittsburgh (a female), wanted to hire yet another female, I found out later. My boss was determined to prove to her boss that he had made a bad decision. And she did.

On the other hand, if you report to the person who brought you on board and it was truly that person's decision to do so, it is in her best interest to make you a success. To return the favor, make sure that your boss looks good in front of her boss. If you are working for the person who selected you, chances are that your personalities mesh. And if you like the boss, chances are that she likes you, too, and that you are similar in many ways. You can propel your careers together.

Take a Part-Time Job

When I was a senior in high school, I was excited to hear that I had been accepted into the radio and television broadcasting program at Ithaca College. I wanted to share the good news with my uncle, a successful orthodontist, who had a second home on the Pacific Ocean, drove a Porsche and was the only college graduate in our extended family.

But Uncle Henry was not pleased to hear the news. "Do you realize," he asked, "that there are more unemployed journalism majors than any other?" Out of fear, I chose a different field of study, but the flame of my interest in broadcasting never stopped flickering.

Twenty years later, as part of my New Year's resolution, I submitted an audio demo tape to a dozen local radio stations. About a month later, I received a call from the general manager at one of the AM stations. "How would you like to do sports on the weekends?" he asked. I was ecstatic! I was able to fulfill a lifetime dream while still keeping my day job. What about you? What else would you like to do? Coach? Sell real estate?

Legal immigrants coming to this country are four times more likely to become millionaires than naturalized citizens are. Why? Because they cannot believe the tremendous opportunities available to them when they come to this country, whereas many of us take them for granted. It's not uncommon to see legal immigrants get a job, take classes in the evenings to improve their English, then also get a part-time job. Then they will save their money and possibly buy a duplex. Based on the proceeds of that investment, they will move into bigger transactions.

The key is that they don't put all of their eggs in one basket. They never think, "If I can just get a six-figure, white-collar job, I'll be on Easy Street." They look to minimize their risks of losing a source of income by having multiple sources of income. My brother Greg is a perfect example. He supplements (and sometimes even exceeds) his regular monthly income by being a Power Seller on eBay.

Moral: By working evenings or weekends, you can dip you toes in the waters of a second career without having to plunge in. It can be a safely net, supplement your income or at least be a nice diversion from your regular work.

Be Financially Lean and Mean

My cousin Barb was on the phone, in tears. After seventeen years with a television news network, she had lost her job when the company merged with another media firm. (Remember my advice earlier in the chapter? Mergers nearly always result in layoffs!)

But it was her concern about something like this happening that had caused Barb to live way below her means—a modest home in an affordable neighborhood and two cars that were both more than a decade old. With her severance package and her savings, Barb would be able to successfully weather the storm of unemployment for a year or even longer.

What about you? Are you like Barb, or are you like many Americans who believe the good times will just continue to roll and believe that a layoff could never happen to them? Some are just two paychecks away from bankruptcy or at least severe financial hardship.

First, do what you can to pay off high-interest, revolving credit card balances. Did you know that if you are only making the minimum monthly payments on a credit card, that it could take you forty years or more to pay off the debt? And that's even if you don't continue to rack up a higher balance. Now you understand why you get so many credit card solicitations in the mail. But which will retire first—you or your credit card debt? (For a lower rate credit card, check out Bankrate.com on the Web.)

> Moral: Being financially lean and mean can allow you to accept contractual work, a temporary cut in pay or take advantage of another opportunity in a new location.

Die Broke

When I mentioned this one day in a seminar, one of my attendees raised his hand to ask me, "Die broke? Why would I want to do that? I read everything I can to help me avoid doing just that!"

"To die broke," I laughed, "means to live life to its fullest. Enjoy your money while you are alive. Just as you shouldn't live just for today by spending beyond your means, neither should you always be sacrificing today for the sake of a tomorrow, which may never come. Treat your family and friends while you can actually see them benefit from your philanthropy. The last check you write should be to the undertaker, and that check should bounce."

This advice comes from the book of the same name written by Stephen M. Pollan and Mark Levine. They also advise, "Most of you will be fired long before you're vested," "Abandon any remaining tinges of loyalty to your employer" and that we should always be looking for a better, higher-paying job.

SO YOU GOT THE PINK SLIP, TOO

Even if you have already been downsized, there are twelve important things to consider.

You are Not Alone!

In the first six months of 2003, nearly 700,000 workers are projected to lose their jobs in layoffs. That's about half of the number of people who work for the nation's largest civilian employer, Wal-Mart.

If you do get laid off, file for unemployment compensation immediately. (I once waited a week, and then lost that week's pay.) Also, check into COBRA health insurance coverage. It can cover you for up to eighteen weeks. Although your employer is required to offer it to you, there's no law that says it has to be offered cheaply.

Face the Facts

I can still remember the day I stood at the window of my office building and watched as some recent layoff casualties, one by one, carried their office belongings to their cars, tearfully hugged surviving co-workers and then drove off. I remember shaking my head and thinking to myself, "Some of them don't even know what they are in for."

Other than my brother-in-law's suicide and my wife being diagnosed with a potentially life-threatening illness, my third layoff was the most traumatic event I have ever experienced. So don't kid yourself. Successfully fighting back from a downsizing will take a lot of hard, frustrating, ego-grinding work.

Expect to go through mood swings. One morning you'll wake up, smile and declare, "I'm so glad to be out of there. Now I'm a free agent. I can do whatever I want." Then you might pull a few more rejection letters out of your mailbox and decide, "No one will ever hire me. I'll never work again!"

Be prepared for other mental adjustments, too. For example, you might enter an interview with a prospective employer and still think of yourself as a six-figure executive. Meanwhile, the interviewer may be thinking, "This is a zero-dollar executive. He or she doesn't have a job."

Some other things you are likely to discover as you go through your job search are that:

- The position is at a lower level in the same industry.
- The company is too far away.
- The benefits aren't the same.
- You'll have to "start over again" in a different industry
- You may be working for someone younger than you for the first time.

Set Your Priorities

How? Take out a piece of paper right now and write down the most important person or thing in your life. What fires you up and gets you out of bed each morning? Repeat this step to identify the second and then the third most critical items. After that, write down how much time you actually spent on each of these three key elements of your life last week.

You will find that this can be a sobering and even painful exercise. As you consider the results, remember that there is never enough time to get everything done—only the important things.

At our Town Hall meetings, the former CEO of my company reminded us that the three priorities in our lives needed to be:

- Faith (whatever we consider that to be)
- Family
- Career

Moral: Recognizing your priorities can help you maintain perspective and give you support, especially when battling back from a downsizing.

Develop a Strategy

This involves first discovering what kind of work you want to do next, then systematically taking the steps that will lead you to your next job.

Your last position may or may not have been ideal (which may have been part of the problem). But now it's time to ask yourself, "What do I want to do for the rest of my life?" Chances are you will find that it has more to do with your passion and your talent than with your years of experience.

I now realize that some of my career problems were the result of my initially accepting others' ideas of what constitutes success. It was hard to accept the fact that my uncle was furious with me for wanting to study broadcast journalism, and had I followed my own heart from the beginning, things may have turned out much differently for me.

In his book, *Finding Work That Matters*, Mark Albion asks, "What did you want to do when you were twelve years old?" Many of us have career aspirations that were squashed early by others when they said, "How are you ever going to make a living doing that?"

My good friend Lisa, who is a very successful sales representative at our company, has the desire and personality to be a compassionate nurse. In fact, she had been going to school part-time to pursue that profession. When she suddenly stopped, I asked why.

"I determined that I could make more money doing what I am doing part time than working full time as a nurse," she replied. So instead, she deals with the stress of her job as well as the stress of not doing what she would really like to do.

We all seem to go through times in our lives when we become what Zig Ziglar so aptly described in his own career as "wandering generalities." In Ziglar's case, he tried deal after deal that didn't work, just as you may have attempted job after job, without giving anything your full commitment. Sales trainer Brian Tracy says that eighty percent of our frustrations in this area can be traced to a lack of clarity.

I remember one of my graduate school classmates being asked what positions he would be interviewing for. His naive reply: "Oh, I want to do MBA work." You'll need to have a better answer than that!

Once you have determined what you would like to do with the rest of your life, develop a spreadsheet that lists:

- What company did I contact?
- With whom did I speak at the company? (name, title, e-mail address, phone number, fax number)
- When did I last reach my contact?
- What is my next action?

Good salespeople are like bloodhounds that are always trying to sniff out the next lead, whether or not they are on the job. To be successful in your job search, you need the same kind of dogged determination:

- Approach companies with which you would like to work in person, by e-mail or by phone.
- Check the classified ads.
- Talk with neighbors, friends, club and church members.
- Take those employed in your desired field out to lunch to obtain advice.
- Be creative—leave no stone unturned.

Realize that what comes around, goes around.

On the evening of my third layoff, I was scheduled to cover a high school basketball game for a radio station where I was working part time. Because of the funk I was in, however, I thought about ditching the assignment. Then I determined that, despite the setback, I was going to try to live my life as normally as possible. So I went to the game.

While I was there, I ran into my friend and (recently) former co-worker, Jim. I remember my humiliation as I relayed to Jim that I had gotten the boot earlier that day. Four years later, Jim and I again meet at a high school basketball game. At that point I had been working for that same company again for nearly three years while Jim had previously left for a new opportunity. He came up to me that night and said, "I was laid off today." How ironic!

Moral: As they say, this too shall pass. It can be so difficult to project the necessary self-confidence and can-do attitude on an interview when your self-esteem is in the dumpster. Believe me, I know. But do it anyway.

Get a Running Start

Mike, a classmate of mine from graduate school, went to work for a railroad right after graduation. After twenty years on the job, he reached the end of the line, so to speak. Railroads do essential work, and I'm sure that Mike had an impressive resume. But what kind of opportunities do you think the market held for a forty-something, out-of-work railroader?

You'll have the odds in your favor if you look for a job:
- In a growth company
- In a growth industry
- In a growth city

Go Where the Prospects Are

According to a survey published in *National Business Employment Weekly*, sixty-three percent of 1,500 successful job hunters said they found new positions through personal contacts while only two percent got jobs by sending out unsolicited resumes.

Keep a Journal

After my brother-in-law died of a self-inflicted gunshot wound, my sister-in-law was devastated. At the suggestion of a therapist, she began to write down descriptions of the feelings that tormented her. "Compare what you have written after three weeks, three months, three years," the therapist advised. "Then you'll have evidence of the healing process."

When I was given my third pink slip, I also kept a journal, which became the basis for two published articles.

James Pennebaker, a research psychologist at the University of Texas at Austin says, "Employees who are fired or laid off and write about their anger, fear and frustration are reemployed more quickly than those who bottle their feelings. Repressing emotions is hard psychological work, but if you release those emotions, the entire body benefits."

Moral: Women may write in their diaries, but real men keep journals!

Your New Full-Time Job

You will find that as you are enduring your (hopefully brief) period between jobs, it will be very tempting for your spouse or significant other to call out to you as he or she heads off to work, "Honey, as long as you're home today, could you pick up the dry cleaning (take the kids over to soccer practice, run that antique chair over to my mother's house, etc.)?"

Willing to do anything other than experience yet another round of rejections, you will be tempted to reply (with your tail wagging and your tongue hanging out), "Sure thing!" But don't. Approach the process of getting a new job as a full-time job in itself. Overcome the temptation of being distracted by daytime television or mundane chores. This "administrivia" can cause you to lose focus on your true goal.

As a diversion, allow yourself to do contractual work, get a part-time job, volunteer or work for a temporary agency, but spend the rest of the time seeking your next position. While I was battling my fifty-seven days of unemployment, I would conduct my job searches in the mornings, then reward myself by going in to the radio station to work in the afternoons.

Moral: Don't spend your time majoring in the minors.

Your Former Company

Stay on good terms with your former co-workers, including your old boss. Why? Although you may not want to come back to join the old office water cooler crowd, you'll still need references for your new employer. Send a letter to your old company saying what a super experience it was to work there. The letter will likely end up in your personnel file and reflect favorably on you when anyone needs to pull out your information for a reference check.

Another reason: Whether they get fired or not, the people you worked with will move on to jobs at other companies with more opportunities.

Moral: Maybe you can be too thin, but you can never have enough money or enough friends.

Your New Company

Approach your new company with the attitude of "This is what I can do for you" rather than "What can you do for me?"

Whenever I give a seminar on downsizing, leadership, how to motivate your employees, sales training or public speaking, I always bring along a portable radio. "Do you realize," I'll begin, "that we all listen to the same radio station? You may find that hard to believe, after hearing what your spouse, children or parents tune in. But we really do. The call letters for that station are WIIFM. They stand for 'What's In It For Me?' And we listen to that station all day long."

I recently took a course on effective business writing. For the first exercise, we were asked to write a memo to the boss to ask for a day off. The typical memos generated by our class said something to the effect of, "Boss, the stress around here is killing me," or "Boss, I have some things around the house or with the kids that I just have to get done." Guess what? The boss doesn't care!

By the end of the course, we had learned how to give the correct response: "Boss, you know how productive I am. Well, if I could just have a day off to take care of some things that could negatively affect my performance, I'd come back supercharged!" Now that's something the boss can listen to because there's something in it for him.

When I want to talk with my seventeen-year-old son, Stephen, he'll quickly tune in his favorite station and roll his eyes if I begin by saying, "I remember when I was your age. I could have bought a new car for just $5,000." Instead, I know now to look him in the eye and discuss the latest video game developments—his area of interest.

WIIFM. It's the secret to getting along with your interviewer, your boss, your employees, your audience, your kids, the restaurant maitre d', your date or your spouse. What is a practical way to put it into motion? Try eliminating the word "I" from your speech and writing and substituting the word "you."

In reality, nobody is ever going to care more about you than you do. And you will never care more about someone else than yourself. But if you can move in the direction of caring about someone else, and if you can effectively convey that concern, you can be successful in any endeavor. People will want to know how much you care before they care how much you know.

> Moral: As Zig Ziglar often states, "You can get anything in this life you want if you can give enough other people what they want."

Product Management

Many people approach the writing of their resume as though they were going through the tedious motions of putting together a shopping list for a trip to the store.

Don't. Instead, think of yourself as a product. (Remember "Me, Inc.?") And at the same time, you are the manager of that product. Your resume is not an irrelevant, disconnected narrative of things you have done on the job. It is your advertisement.

Composing Your Resume

It's not unusual for people who have been recently laid off to lament, "I sent out 500 resumes and didn't get a single interview." Are times really that tough? Maybe we shouldn't be sending out resumes at all!

In his book of the same name, Jeffrey J. Fox suggests, "Don't send a resume." Instead, he states that you should send a customized letter to the highest-level person who could hire you in your prospective organization. Only after you get the interview should you follow up with an individualized resume.

Top-notch salespeople will position their sales materials and highlight only those product features that translate into benefits for a particular prospect. Beginning salespeople, on the other hand, are likely to do a generalized data dump when they walk through the door, hoping that something (anything) will catch the attention of the potential customer.

I once sold software for my current company, so it was interesting in a later position with the company to be the potential purchaser of other companies' software. The less skilled salespeople would display all of their product literature and say, "This is what my software can do. Tell me if any of this would fit what you want to do." On the other hand, the stellar salespeople would begin by saying, "Let's discuss your needs first, then I can determine if my product can actually help you."

How long do you have to grab the attention of the recipient of your resume? Twenty seconds? If you make it hard on her, you may have ten seconds or less to impress her. Remember, she doesn't care about what you've done. She only wants to know what you could do for her.

Tackling Your Interview

It's moments before the event of reckoning—your interview. Let's take a look at the person in the hot seat—your interviewer. That's right, your interviewer! You see, for you this interview may be just another step on your path to employment nirvana. But for the interviewer, this move might make or break her career.

Before you enter, she is thinking, "I can't believe how many applicants have virtually ignored Bobbie, our receptionist. They even seem to think of me as just some kind of conduit to the job. Don't they realize that companies don't hire people—people hire people? I need to make sure that I keep the good chemistry around here.

"And how about the ones who ask, 'What does your company do?' Haven't they ever heard of the Internet? Or the ones who want to know about pay, hours, vacation and other benefits. They don't even have the job yet!

"Maybe that last person was a little nervous, but he just went on and on about all the scholastic and academic awards he received. Thought he walked on water. Doesn't he know that the way to make others think he's great is to first make them feel great about themselves?"

How can you make a better impression than the ones made by these other interviewees—*and* get the job? You have your choice of two objectives:

1. Find the interviewer's pain, and show how you can take it away.

or

2. Figure out what you can do for your interviewer that the others can't do or hadn't thought of doing.

To get you started, ask my favorite interviewing question:

"You obviously have been quite successful with the company. To what do you attribute your success?"

Then lean forward, cock your head slightly and let the interviewer speak while you listen with genuine interest.

What you will find, first of all, is that the interviewer will be surprised. Finally, someone has given her the opportunity to speak. And not about the company either but about herself. Rarely will any candidate show such a personal interest. She will be flattered!

Second, the interviewer will reveal, through her own experience, what she is looking for in a candidate. For example, if she states that she has achieved success by working harder and smarter than anyone else in the department, you will want to demonstrate how you have been able to mirror this behavior in your own career when it is your turn to speak. As we discussed earlier, people like people who are just like themselves.

I used this technique to gain a plane ticket to my first on-site interview. The representative from the company who had been sent to talk to me on campus had such a good time regaling me with stories of his college experience, I barely had the chance to get in a word. But after he had concluded his last chuckle, he declared, "I believe you are just the kind of person we want working for our firm!"

Do you ever have discussions with your spouse or a close friend in which you can instinctively tell they haven't bought in to what you have told them? Do you then just walk away? No, you read their body language and ask them something like, "What's the matter?" In that way, you get another chance to make sure that you are understood and can gain agreement.

Similarly, near the end of your interview, ask:

"Is there anything that would keep you from hiring me?"

This allows you a final opportunity to overcome any objections that may be lurking in the back of the interviewer's mind. If you don't address it now, you won't be around later to shoot it down when it threatens to destroy your chances at the job.

The best salespeople always assume closing the sale and thus act accordingly. Since your interview is simply a sales call (you are selling "Me, Inc."), be sure to do the same. Ask:

"What is the next step?"

The cardinal rule among public speakers is that you can violate any of the other commonly accepted rules about speaking, except one—

showing passion for your topic. If you don't have an extreme interest in your subject, your audience won't forgive you.

Likewise, at the end of your interview, say:

"I'm excited about the job. I want it. May I have it?"

In response, your interviewer may laugh and say that he or she must first talk with others. But this response will demonstrate your confidence and passion, essential ingredients for success in any job that the other candidates may be lacking.

Your interview may be completed, but your selection process is probably just beginning. In fact, it may extend for several weeks or months. Even if you are behind in this game, you still have plenty of chances to score points.

I really had no business interviewing for my current company. I had been a pharmaceutical salesperson for the previous half dozen years, so what could I possibly know about computers? And originally, I didn't get the job. Instead, my company decided to hire somebody who was already in the business of selling computer hardware. So how did I get the job? To keep myself fresh in the mind of my future boss, Brenda, I did the following:

- Sent her articles of interest from trade journals she may not have had the chance to read
- Left thirty-second infomercials on her voicemail after hours
- Kept her abreast of any ongoing sales achievements I had earned

I was rejected in July of that year, but by September, the person they originally hired left the company, and I had an offer from Brenda. Nine years later, I am still with the same company.

As you drive home from your interview, it is easy to imagine that all the subsequent candidates for the position scored perfect 1600 scores on their SAT tests and are now brilliant scholars, having graduated from Stanford University with their Ph.D.s. What can you do to help dispel these images from your mind? You can begin to productively channel your interest by immediately writing a thank-you note. In addition to thanking the interviewer for her time, the note will reiterate:

- Why you want the job
- What impact you could have on the company
- Your key competitive strengths
- Something you may have wanted to say during the interview but didn't

Negotiating the Offer

My brother Greg was on the phone line. "I got the offer!" he said, "But..."

"But what?" I replied.

"I wish it was for a bit more money. But I'm afraid to ask for more because I'm afraid they'll just take the offer away."

"Greg," I said, "This is the one time when you truly have some leverage with your employer. They just went though an extensive process to select you. In their minds, you are number one! You have a halo around your head! This is the time to ask for more money. Your employer doesn't want to blow it, either. Do you think that they want to spend several thousand dollars to continue the process for several more weeks? Do you think they want to go back to another candidate on their knees and say, 'Our first choice turned us down. Will you take the job?'"

Greg laughed. I asked him, "Did you have anything else in the works?"

"Well, yes," he replied. "But this is the job I really want!"

"Okay, go back to the person who made you the offer and say, 'I appreciate your confidence in me and would really like to work for you. But I am also considering another opportunity. Could you do anything to make my choice easier?'"

After investing in just several minutes of conversation with his new boss, Greg got the job he wanted and several thousand more dollars in his starting salary. Best of all, he will continue to get annual percentage increases in pay, based on an already higher base salary.

A Final Word—on Rejection

You'll also need to learn to not take post-interview rejection personally. While this is easy to say, it's often hard to do. A rejection after an interview simply means that someone believes that you cannot provide enough economic value to the company at that point in time.

My brother James had followed all of the rules that you have read in this chapter and most of the others you will find in this book. But he was stunned when he didn't get an offer. For his next interview, James was purposely nonchalant. He didn't even bother to cut his hair. But he and the interviewer just clicked, and James got the job.

People are not inherently logical beings. We use logic to back up our emotions, not the other way around. If you are rejected, remember what sales trainer Brian Tracy says: "Opportunities are like buses. If you have patience, another will eventually come along."

Rejection as the result of an interview does not reflect on your true value as a person. Remember that you are a valuable human being. You are not your job. And no matter how you slice it, what you are going after is only a job.

Ted Janusz

Ted Janusz understands current, real-world business challenges, like having to constantly do more with less. In addition to operating his own speaking and training company, Janus Presentations, Ted is currently a full-time Sales Training Program Manager with Sterling Commerce in Dublin, Ohio. Ted has experienced the constant change at Sterling Commerce, an international electronic commerce software and services provider, since he began working there in 1994. Ted is a member of the National Speakers Association, the National Speakers Association of Ohio and has earned his MBA in Marketing from the University of Pittsburgh. He is a former professional entertainer, having performed at over 400 events. Through Janus Presentations, Ted's most requested topics are: "How to Profit from the Upcoming Recovery," "You CAN Recover from a Downsizing," "Customer-Focused Selling" and "How to Keep Your Good Employees." Among Ted's regular clients are the Ohio Society of CPAs and the Midwest Dental Implant Institute. A dynamic, insightful, humorous and down-to-earth presenter, Ted Janusz is welcomed by businesses all across the United States.

Ted Janusz
Janus Presentations
5467 Hyde Park Drive
Hilliard, OH 43026-8582
(614) 527-9294
Email: tjanusz@att.net

Chapter 4

Career Trends: Opening the Door to Hot Jobs in Today's Economy

Debbie Christofferson, CISSP, CISM

What are the hot jobs today? What are the key trends in the environment affecting them, and what do they mean? What's the impact to businesses and how they manage their workforce development programs?

The dot-com crash, telecommunications overcapacity, the fall of industry leaders, a slowed technology sector and an economic downturn have changed the market forever. And while "Here today and gone tomorrow" will still be a common refrain, many businesses and industries will grow and thrive nonetheless. Hot industries and jobs can emerge from any market, and every economy has its opportunities. Today's economic climate is no exception. For instance, some of Arizona's mines have started to operate again, thanks to the substantial rise in the price of gold, which has been driven by a depressed stock market and world uncertainty.

According to a 2002 Brainbench article on Monster.com, many employers fail to achieve the levels of productivity that would make them profitable. Their workers lack needed training and never reach their full potential. Employers must understand the trends and pursue the needs of their workforces for continuous education, retraining and upgrading of skills.

Today's job market is nothing like yesterday's. Education is a requirement as are specific soft skills required in any job setting. Certifications offer competitive strategy on both sides of the fence. To focus yourself and leverage today's opportunities, you must know the trends, what they mean and how to apply them to your own specific situation. You must also know where to find resources to meet your own needs. We'll start by taking a look at the fields creating employment today, look around the corner at trends, then apply them both to workforce training needs.

HOTTEST JOB MARKETS

Major hotbeds of activity in today's job market include healthcare, security, technology and small business. Since our economy is driven by information technology (IT), that field will continue to be predominant, but in different ways. Pockets of opportunity also exist in other professions and locations, reflecting a recent shift toward a service economy.

Healthcare

Healthcare is the highest growth industry, with the most opportunities in sheer volume and with equal increases in positions up, down and across the spectrum. In a recent Phoenix, Arizona, newspaper, job openings accounted for nearly twenty-five percent of the entire Help Wanted section. An aging population, longer life spans and traditional shortages in health care all contribute to this phenomenon. According to last September's SRP Phoenix Economic Forecast, one quarter of all men were projected to be future sufferers of Alzheimer's Disease; and this is just one small example of the challenges ahead.

- Nurses are in high demand, including those needed for heart surgery and allergy and asthma treatment. Many other healthcare opportunities abound as well: physicians, pharmacists, at-home caregivers, billing and coding specialists, nurse practitioners, physician's assistants, dental hygienists, technicians, administrators, managers and even insurance providers.
- Chiropractic is a growing field that's been getting greater recognition. Naturopathy, while a small profession, is also gaining respect, although only twelve U.S. states currently recognize the practice. Naturopaths rely on natural remedies

such as nutrition, vitamins, herbs, counseling, education and physical manipulation to cure illnesses.

- The prominence of gyms and workout facilities, along with a strong focus on health-related products is reflective of our nation's focus on wellness. In the U.S. and abroad, plastic surgery, spas and massage therapy are also growth fields.

Security

While the information technology sector has shrunk considerably, the information security field is one exception that continues to grow and receive funding. This is attributed, in part, to the recently formed Department of Homeland Security, which has pointed a huge spotlight on the entire field of security and threat management.

The increased miniaturization and sophistication of our technology is also leading to more emphasis being placed on the security field. Although wireless technology reflects these advances, inadequate security currently prevents it from being as widely deployed as it should be. However, this is changing as the technology becomes more predominant.

Computer hacking and other cyber crimes have increased substantially in recent years and are expected to explode further as Internet and electronic business grows. Identity theft, fraud and stolen trade secrets are increasingly common. Pirated software, videos and music are easily taken when the opportunities present themselves.

Instant Messaging creates greater avenues for online harassment, resulting in security-aligned privacy concerns and legislation. And, of course, viruses, Trojan horses and worms constitute a plague that is here to stay. They will continue to spread to wireless devices such as pagers, cell phones and PDAs as these services grow.

All of the challenges outlined above will require software, hardware and other countermeasures to keep them from disrupting business. Each has legal ramifications for a company, not to mention the direct negative consequences for the bottom line. This all translates to more jobs in the technology security sector. It also means increased opportunities in network, web site and database management as well as a need for hardware and software developers, administrators and engineers for IT systems.

Virus management is an absolute requirement for computing platforms, and intrusion detection and penetration testing will be a must for networks, servers and computing applications. Biometrics is an emerging field which will simplify facility and computer or network access control. It involves scanning of a physical characteristic to verify the identity of an individual. Biological traits, such as those based on retinal or iris scanning, fingerprints, or facial recognition are used.

Technology

In the Phoenix 2003 Salt River Project Economic Forecast, it was reported that a full third of the U.S. gross domestic product is currently driven by technology. We were cited as the first nation in history to be driven by IT.

The DEMO 2003 iDG Executive Forum is an exclusive conference where new technology products are debuted, giving business leaders an idea of where the industry is headed. This year's Arizona conference focused more on incremental improvements to existing technologies rather than new replacement products and technologies.

The February 16, 2003 edition of the *Arizona Republic* noted these new technology introductions:

- Products that fight e-mail Spam
- Products that make computer networks more secure
- Products that unify communication devices
- Software to help small and emerging companies create or expand online business
- Next-generation technology
- Innovations to jump start technology economy

We are in an era of knowledge, and technology will continue to drive the economy. Technology is big business.

Gartner Inc.'s Dataquest market researchers recently reported projected growth of 8.9 percent in 2003 for worldwide semiconductor sales. The Semiconductor Industry Association (SIA) reported on the Dow Jones that semiconductor sales had previously risen by 1.3 percent in 2002. As an example of the growing optimism, Intel Corporation announced another major investment in the U.S. chip industry, despite the prominence of factory outsourcing. Intel's Arizona factory will be revamped to support state-of-the-art Pentium manufacturing of larger twelve-inch wafers with even tinier transistors.

Computer chips are everywhere and will be used across the board in old and new ways. Tiny chips are being implanted in animals by veterinarians to help identify and return lost pets, and the *Wall Street Journal* reported recently that Nevada's Lake Mead National Recreation Area, in a novel use of the technology, is implanting computer chips in certain cactus species to help track down stolen plants. It seems that this type of theft is burgeoning in the Southwest, where water conservation and desert landscaping create high cactus demand.

All kinds of electronics depend on chips, such as kitchen appliances and mobile data units in police cars. Even at Germany's Volkswagen automotive theme park, a solid IT infrastructure underlies the operations of that state-of-the-art facility.

Smart software tools are being developed to better manage computing tasks, such as control of e-mail volume. There is also a lot of room for growth in productivity improvement tools like online collaboration and information sharing technology. Language translation will be a software requirement in our global economy, and even the heyday of video game software developers will continue; the industry is booming.

Information Technology

IT is a major driver of the economy in the U.S., and the world economy depends on it. It is used to run companies, take orders, ship products, keep a factory running and operate nearly every aspect of a business. Few companies can operate without information technology. It offers a competitive advantage, and even with downsizing, the need for technology skills and workers will not go away; it will simply change. Computing is pervasive, more devices are sharing information with each other, and networks are growing larger and smarter.

Most IT skills today are related to the Internet. Jobs that run the infrastructure and are in demand today include:

- Network administration
- Database administration
- C and C++ programming
- Security management and administration
- E-commerce skills
- Internet transactions and applications
- Internet infrastructure (network design, implementation and support)
- Web development administration
- Java development
- Telecommunications specialization (state-of-the-art complex phone systems)
- System administration

UNIX programming and administration is still a mainstay because UNIX is the operating system for much of today's network infrastructure. Although very popular on its own, LINUX is included here as a version of UNIX.

Training and Education

- Educating our future generations is important, and this will create an ongoing demand for teachers. Teaching specialties include elementary, social studies, math, science, special education and bilingual (particularly Spanish). Teachers are in the highest demand in rural towns and in cities near Mexican border areas. School superintendents are also in short supply.

- Some growth fields have become responsible for creating their own pools of workers through job-specific education opportunities. For example, bartending schools have benefited from the economic downturn, according to the October 14, 2002 edition of *Business Week*. Enrollments have risen thanks to an influx of displaced workers from suffering industries. Bartenders are recession-proof and needed in any economy, particularly when slumps stimulate their demand.

- Massage therapy training is another growing educational field, and disk jockey training enrollment has also increased. *Fortune* magazine reported in October 2002 that there is money to be made teaching people how to use DJ equipment. In the U.S. alone, this is a $500 million business.

- E-Learning—or online, web-based training—is one education medium with a lot of growth potential. Businesses are using it to reduce travel and training costs, and individuals are using it for more flexibility in their education and work schedules. Self-paced training isn't always effective, but the market will continue to evolve and is here to stay.

Business Coaching

Coaching is a young and fast-growing profession, with its own certification and training bodies. Categories of business coaches include life strategists as well as coaches for executives, businesses, careers, leadership, speaking and book authoring. Coaching is conducive to a home office setup, 24-7 availability and flexibility, and virtual clients who can be reached by e-mail or telephone—anytime, anyplace—to develop potential and results.

The collapse of the stock market (and many a fortune) has meant that more people are also seeking advice and guidance from financial planners.

Small Business and Start-ups

The number of self-employed workers in the U.S. declined last year, and venture capital funding was limited. But a recent *U.S.A Today* study touted a sixty-seven-percent success rate for recent start-up businesses. These numbers show that entrepreneurship is still alive and well at a time when we need it most. Previous numbers stated that ninety percent of new start-ups failed in the first year, but this figure may be inaccurate since it was based on all business closures; however, not all closures are related to failure.

More and more people are also discovering the advantages of working a home-based business. Working at home gives owners more flexibility and lowers start-up costs. Desktop publishing, financial advising, business coaching, seminar leaders, copywriters, professional speakers, technical writers, real estate professionals, insurance claim processing, insurance agent, and professional organizer include some of the possibilities.

The Youth Market

This demographic has lots of spending power, and as a result is the target of more and more businesses and marketing campaigns. This market tops $155 billion annually in retail spending, according to numbers in a November 2002 *Arizona Republic* article. Be aware that the fickle nature of the youth market can take your business up or down, but it can also offer unique opportunities.

Home Construction

As interest rates in our country have remained at historic lows and mortgage rates have held at the lowest point in four decades, new home construction has boomed. The Associated Press reported new home starts as being at their highest levels since 1986. This impacts all manner of industries and employment—mortgage brokers, appraisers, real estate agents, lenders, construction project estimators and superintendents, inspectors and heavy equipment rentals, to name only a few. There is no bubble in most markets. Although this trend could shift if the interest rates change, no long-term slowdown is anticipated in 2003. Commercial properties are in a slump in the economy, however, and that won't pick up for another two years.

Law Enforcement

Crime rises in a sluggish economy. This creates staffing needs in law enforcement and detention facilities. In addition to police and court officers, workers needed include counselors, social workers, legal advisors, identification technicians, detention officers and kitchen, cleaning and laundry staff, to mention a few. Cities close to prisons must also create opportunities for the released population to integrate into the community and workforce. Unfortunately, though, government spending is typically reduced in a down economy, and creative cost-cutting is a fact of life.

TRENDS

A number of different trends will have an impact on both current and future job markets, including emergency and outsourcing markets.

Information Technology

Living in a globally connected world means that the Internet will continue to play a significant role in our lives and in the job market. Therefore, technology will remain a driver in this current era of knowledge.

Summarizing three different studies, *Computerworld* magazine reported some conflicting numbers when it comes to future IT spending. A Sacks-Goldman study, for example, predicted a handful of increases in spending but that the overall IT market was still trending downward. Nevertheless, watch for a five percent increase in manufacturing IT spending, compared to a sixteen percent drop the previous year. Although communications spending is estimated to decline by twelve percent, this outlook is still much more favorable than the thirty-six percent decline experienced in 2002.

Globally, Sacks-Goldman results identified the looming dominance of security products and wireless Local Area Network (LAN) technology (the federal government anticipates increased spending in both sectors). Enterprise portal software and upgrades of Microsoft Windows operating systems were other areas of the study's focus.

Identity theft and fraud are expected to spur security technology. Likewise, regulation of the health and finance industries mandating privacy, confidentiality and integrity will drive security and oversight investment—and litigation. The Internet's economic impact and use will only compound security needs.

Wireless technology, which should continue to experience global growth, will feature new devices with multiple access points. Increased wireless connectivity will mean that technology solutions are required for security, authorization and identification software, network protection and anti-virus software. This type of security will require encryption, firewalls, digital certificates, public key infrastructure and intrusion detection and correction systems.

Threat reduction in the U.S. is creating demand on many fronts. Both public and private enterprises are expanding their security infrastructures, resulting in increased security personnel and medical response activities. (While the Internet will continue to expand its presence in the travel and airline industries, these sectors have, nonetheless, been decimated by the economy and the current global environment. Some will retrench, although others will never recover.)

Disaster recovery and contingency planning spending will be up. The federal government will increase IT spending to support the added focus on security infrastructure and to simplify and consolidate systems and services.

Engineering industries will be required to neutralize and eliminate chemical and other weapons in the United States, Russia and possibly some countries in the Middle East. Numerous rebuilding efforts such as bridge building, road repair and land mine removal must also take place following war.

Network system processing will increase the need for storage and administration as well as the utilities to manage it all (Linux, for example, will see a large growth in server sales as it makes more inroads into that market). Arrays of specialized servers will support network-based computing and storage. The storage capacities will be large, fostering further integration between companies and their partners. Network bandwidths will increase, and standards will become more open with less proprietary systems.

According to Intel Corporation's Gordon Moore, the growth in the density and performance of microprocessors could be maintained for another eight to twelve years. Computer chips continue to shrink and are finding their way into all types of appliances, including kitchen countertops. An immature telephone and network infrastructure offers lots of room for microprocessor growth in developing countries like China and Mexico.

As reported by the Dow Jones in February 2003, the Semiconductor Industry Association anticipates increased spending on IT hardware this year. This is attributable to the momentum of cell phone and personal computer sales and the return of the corporate buyer to the market (incidentally, Asia and the Pacific rim are the world's largest and fastest growing markets).

Overall, IT decisions will be driven more by a service economy. Computer support offerings to customers will increase, and help desk capability will be more automated. Outsourcing will account for a larger percentage of IT budgets, supporting both the contract employee workforce trend and cost management.

But don't hold your breath for a total IT recovery in 2003. IT managers are pessimistic about spending, which slows companies' revenues and profitability, and IT spending likely will never return to 1990s levels. But IT workers will remain in demand nonetheless, and the global trends and issues we've highlighted will drive the market.

Emerging Countries

India, China and Eastern Europe are already impacting the global job market as factories, engineering design, service centers and information technology are outsourced from the United States, Western Europe and Japan. Even Mexico is affected as its factories shift operations to Asia.

On the other hand, emerging economies will open up new markets for PCs and other technology, products and services since salaries and disposable incomes have increased in these countries. By 2005, China will be the largest growing marketplace for U.S. entrepreneurs because it has the fastest growth in Internet users.

Outsourcing and Contract Employment

While owning one's own career is not a new term, contract employment is certainly the new wave of the current and future workforce. This is especially true in today's IT market. Technology skills will still be important in these outsourcing programs as will the opportunities to manage them.

The outsourcing trend will continue as companies look to reduce costs and gain more efficiency in remote management. While this affords opportunities in emerging economies, it affects the job market adversely in places where jobs are being lost. Companies will have to look at their operations differently and learn where their base employees can add the most value, both to the core business and research and development.

Diversity

As the Internet brings us all closer together, the ability to speak and translate multiple languages is a growing need. Growth of the Hispanic population has been huge, which is leading to its predominance in the U.S. market. Arizona's SRP 2003 forecast stated that as much as forty percent of the state's population growth in the 1990s was accounted for by Hispanics.

For immigrants to thrive, learning English as a second language will be needed to gain employment. Ethnically diverse workforces then create new markets for more specialized products and services that are targeted toward these different cultures.

For example, in her 2003 State of the City address, the mayor of Cleveland, Ohio, described that city as "a melting pot of opportunity." People from 116 countries call it home, she added, noting the fact that great cities have been built on the talents and hard work of immigrants.

On the flipside of the diversity issue, however, Illegal immigration in some locations was thought to create a drag on wages last year. This is because a large migrating population may lack the opportunities to compete for higher paying jobs and can put a strain on any city, state or federal government infrastructure.

Biotechnology

Bioscience research and development facilities are being created, resulting in huge growth and career opportunities today and in the decades to come. All manner of research will go on in the medical and bioscience fields to create solutions for our society's health problems, which, consequently, is beneficial to our future. Stem cell regeneration is only one of many opportunities to be explored, in addition to the convergence of both biotech and nontech manipulation.

Saving Natural Resources

Energy, fuel and water will be in shorter supply, requiring conservation efforts worldwide. Fuel cell development will be an area of growth as will the "green" movement to preserve the Earth and its resources.

Airline Industry

The U.S. airline industry requires improvement in the areas of efficiency and labor costs. Otherwise, it will leave a littered graveyard among the ranks of the major carriers, creating a negative ripple affect in related industries. The *Wall Street Journal* expounded on this in a recent analysis of United Airlines, detailing how economic and global woes have brought the crisis to the forefront. Pay, benefits and competition cease to be a factor when a company and its jobs disappear into the night. For the sake of the economy, tourism and the travel industry, the hope is for reinvention. Service and employee morale must also be maintained to operate the airline and keep customers. Old ways of thinking won't provide a solution.

The Space Program

Despite a recent space shuttle disaster and compression in the aerospace industry, the *Wall Street Journal* reported in February that NASA still lacks adequate numbers of skilled workers. Science and engineering student enrollment is declining. And an aging industry workforce and a corresponding shortage of specialists in areas such as robotics and propulsion will take a huge toll in ten years. More talent is required.

Aging Population

An aging population will not only impact health care but shift workforce dynamics completely. Benefits costs will rise, but businesses must change the way the workforce is hired, managed and grown. This is true not only in the U.S. but in Japan and Europe.

According to Amy Schurr, writing in the August 2002 *Network World Newsletter*, approximately sixty million Baby Boomers will be leaving the workforce in the next fifteen years, creating huge manpower shortages. This means that more people will be leaving the workforce than entering it. Baby Boomers are also the largest population demographic and have the largest concentration of wealth and spending power as a market.

Convenience

Time is money. Convenience sells if you're marketing or creating a product or service. And busy children, long commutes and hectic work schedules mean that convenience will continue to sell. Doing housework and cooking are simply not how people want to spend their limited free time, a fact substantiated by a recent A.C. Nielsen survey.

Microwave ovens turned out to be just the beginning of faster, easier lives. Items like new wet-dry mops with disposable pads and wet wipes for cleaning children, glass or furniture will remain popular.

Prepackaged convenience foods are big sellers, too, and run the gamut from easy-fix items and completely prepared meals in the grocer's freezer to cubed cheeses, pre-made appetizer trays and meals delivered to the home.

EDUCATION AND SOFT SKILLS

Today's information-driven economy requires more and more knowledgeable workers. Education will be critical, and a high school diploma will no longer be enough.

Degrees translate into real money, and specialists in any field will be in higher demand. An MBA, for example, leads to a wide choice of career paths, with an equally wide variety of salaries. The October/November 2002 issue of *Executive Female* cited a Census Bureau study that showed lifetime earnings of doctoral or professional degree holders to be four times that of high school graduates. An earning differential also applies to holders of master's and bachelor's degrees, although the margin isn't quite as wide.

"Soft" skills, like effective communication, teamwork and adaptability will also be crucial when it comes to competing in the ever-changing marketplace.

Certifications

Certification demonstrates an employee's knowledge and skill foundation, and it has the ability to increase pay and career opportunities. In addition to verifying a base level of knowledge and competence, a certification also shows an employee's commitment to continuing education. To maintain a certification, a person's knowledge must be current and maintained in the future.

Certification will be a differentiator—a hiring requirement in some fields—as a competitive advantage for job seekers and as an opportunity for increased compensation or career growth. From the employer's standpoint, certifications pay for themselves when you have employees working in roles that fit their career paths.

But while a certification can and does demonstrate a given level of competence in an area, its validity depends on the specific certification, which determines the worker's value to the employer. Not all are certifications are created equal; some are valued most in a tight market or start-up environment (the early Microsoft Certified System Engineer, for example).

Many businesses seek workers with highly specialized certifications, and more jobs are requiring them, including the IT security and networking fields. The CISSP certification, which applies to enterprise security management, is one of the most sought-after today. It requires knowledge and experience in the field in addition to passing and maintaining certification requirements. Enterprise software certifications for specific products are also common and in demand for shops running systems from specific vendors.

WORKFORCE TRAINING NEEDS

No business is viable without its human capital—the employees. But many businesses cut or eliminate training when a downturn occurs, and today is no exception. Continuous learning is a requirement in any economy and for any position. Employers and their staffs must be creative in finding ways to stay educated.

Employers are putting the costs of new skill training back on employees as one way to save money, since it's the employee's responsibility to gain the skills needed to compete. This may work in the short run, but even in a down market, the tide will always change, and if they feel they aren't valued, employees will bolt when the tide shifts in their favor.

Businesses will need employees with cutting-edge skills as new technologies and market conditions arrive. Employers must prepare by developing or buying the skills needed to run their businesses productively and profitably. Whenever possible, it's best to build a skill internally, rather than hiring outside. Current employees always know more about a business than newcomers.

In addition to classes, seminars and trade conferences, there are multiple ways to developing necessary skills, including online courses, self-paced tutorials, books, trade magazines, mentoring, shadowing, special interest groups, master groups, college classes or telecasts. If a worker has a particular cutting-edge skill, he or she might be able to translate it into a training manual or into seminar format to help share that knowledge with other staff members.

Employers can also offer workers a career development plan that meets both the employees' needs and those of the business. Opportunities can be plentiful for each employee, regardless of interests and skills.

If you are a manager, you should develop a contingency plan to replace the skills of staff members who are critical to the operation. This includes rotating your staff according to their interests and building a succession plan for the management team. Also, identify the job skills and positions you need and make sure you have enough depth in your staff to cover the business adequately. Special projects can routinely be staffed this way as your business requirements ebb and flow.

Review your plan every year, and adjust it for current market conditions and trends as well as the skills your staff needs to help your business succeed. A down market is no time to take short cuts; you must continue to plan for tomorrow.

SUMMARY

If you have a big hat and no cattle, as they say in Texas, you're out. The weak will be weeded out of the economy. Technology and the Internet will stay mainstream with pervasive collaborative networks that make the Internet transparent. The infrastructure, businesses, and employees must be flexible and scalable. Collaboration and innovation will drive competitive advantage and future value. Business will be customer-driven, so the customer experience will be important. Only the future will reveal the new technology that will change our lives tomorrow.

Debbie Christofferson, CISSP, CISM

Debbie Christofferson holds 20 years management experience in Fortune 500 companies, and 25 years in the high-tech industry. Debbie explores trends and applies them to the job market and career opportunities. She has worked in Asia, Europe, and the U.S., and understands the macro business view. She speaks and writes from life experience. Debbie's last dozen years have focused on information security, and she holds one of the most valued security certifications, in one of the hottest job fields, the CISSP (Certified Information Security Systems Professional). Based on her IT security management expertise, Debbie offers consulting, risk and security assessments, reports, project management, staff development and hiring guidance, customized training, speaking, speech writing, and articles. She resides in Arizona, and is available for global assignments. Debbie is a consultant, speaker, and writer.

Debbie Christofferson
Sapphire Security Services
P.O. Box 11913
Tempe, AZ 85284-0032
(480) 988-4194, Office
(877) 471-0548, Fax
Web: www.career-therapy.com
Email: DebbieChristofferson@earthlink.net

Chapter 5

Social Skills Can Mean Business Success

Lydia Ramsey

Robert and Barbara are business professionals in their mid 30s, with similar educational and career experience. They work in an industry that affords them both opportunities for advancement. However, Robert's career has hit a snag while Barbara is climbing the corporate ladder at a nice pace. Why is one stuck on a lower rung while the other is making a smooth ascent? What are the factors that are contributing to the success of one and the apparent lack of it for the other? In many cases, the stumbling blocks are subtle and simple, things that seem almost trivial yet play a major part in the success saga of every person in the business world. Some people deal with these career issues naturally. Others toss them aside as "old school" or inconsequential. In reality, people who achieve lasting success have a heightened understanding of these principals and practices and diligently strive to increase their mastery of them. These are the people who understand the importance of relationships in business, and these are the people who trouble themselves to understand and to sharpen their personal skills in the professional environment.

Business success is based on many factors. Most people think that getting ahead depends on education, expertise and experience. While all of these are necessary for a certain level of achievement, they will do you no good if you can't relate to other people in the business arena. Getting ahead is truly a matter of getting along.

All things being equal, people tend to do business with people they like. All things not being equal, people tend to do business with people they like. And people like people who make them feel comfortable and at ease. Some people seem naturally confident with others; but the real truth is that in this world of introverts and extroverts, none of us is born knowing how to get along with others. Think of a room full of four-year-olds. It's not exactly a civilized scene. The teacher is there not only to educate and keep order but also to teach everyone the rules for getting along with each other. Our social skills are learned behaviors. Like all other skills, they need practice to become perfect.

Every business day will provide opportunities for you to showcase your social skills. There are encounters in and out of the office where you are called upon to interact with customers, clients, colleagues and co-workers. Some of these occasions seem purely business-oriented, such as meetings and appointments. Others seem more social, like the after-hours reception or the client dinner. However, every business encounter has an element of social interaction attached to it. Some are just more obvious than others. For the purpose of this chapter, we will focus on those occasions that on the surface seem to be more of a social rather than a business nature. How you act and interact with others in an out-of-office environment is often the key factor in whether you land a job, get a promotion or seal a deal.

There Are No Second Chances to Make a First Impression

It all starts with the first impression. Most people know the clichés: "The first impression is the lasting one" and "You never get a second chance to make a first impression." What few people consider is that the first impression can occur any time and any place, meaning that no matter where you are or what you are doing, you have to be ready at all times for that initial and critical encounter with the would-be employer, client or business connection. It could be at a business meeting, a community luncheon or the fresh produce section of your local grocery store.

If your first impression is going to be your most positive and professional, then it is important to know what elements are critical when you meet someone for the first time. If you are encountering a person face to face, be aware that fifty-five percent of how you will be judged is based on what the other person sees. The other forty-five percent is based on the words that you say. Amazingly, only seven percent depends on the actual words themselves. Thirty-eight percent of how people judge you is by the tone of your voice. So if you are doing the math, ninety-three percent of how you are perceived comes from non-verbal information.

All of this happens in an instant. It only takes between three and seven seconds to form an opinion. We'd like to think that we don't judge others by their appearances, but in truth, we do. In the first few seconds of a personal encounter, the only information we have is visual. We look the other person in the face and form an opinion based on what we see from the neck up. That means that personal grooming of the face and hair sends the strongest signals. You really can't afford to have a bad hair day. Some days are better than others for all us, but we always have to give it our best effort. So don't put off that haircut or the color job when the roots start to show. That's the day you'll run right into the person you have been trying to get an appointment with for months.

For women, makeup application is a factor. Too much make-up is inappropriate in business and will make you stand out from the crowd for all the wrong reasons. Too little sends a message that you don't value other people enough to spend time making yourself attractive. For men, it's facial hair and how it is managed that catches the eye. From the neck up, other considerations are jewelry, scarves, collars and necklines. All of these factors enter into what others think of us at first blush and whether we appear to be professional, competent and, yes, even appealing.

The next place the eye travels in the first few seconds is to the feet. In fact, after working with countless people on first impressions, I have concluded that there is a totally heretofore-unrecognized group of people; they are the "shoe people." They notice shoes first, and they form judgments based upon what they see on other peoples' feet. Shoes that are well maintained and appropriate for the business environment send a positive message. If a person fails to appreciate the appearance of his shoes, he is likely to be seen as someone who doesn't pay attention to detail in business.

Hemlines for both pants and skirts are noticed, as are socks and stockings. Skirts should be no more than two inches above the knee, and an overly long skirt detracts from a professional presence. The length of pants is as important for women as it is for men. There should be a slight break of the hemline over the top of the foot. Don't make the mistake of wearing pants that are too short and look as if you pulled them up too far. Socks should always match not just what you are wearing but each other; and stockings are essential for the professional woman.

Although what you say only makes up a mere seven percent of how others assess you, the first words that come out of your mouth will affect what people think. Offer an immediate "thank you." "Thank you for taking your time to see me today," or whatever appreciation is appropriate. Next use the other person's name within the first few seconds. Think how good you feel when someone calls you by name and make the effort to include names in conversation from the start.

Whatever else you say within those first few seconds is not nearly as important as the way that you say it. Pay attention to your tone of voice. A pleasant tone is heard above all else. That simple phrase "Have a nice day" can sound like either a pleasant wish or a veiled threat.

Ready, Set, Shake Hands

Handshakes are involved in virtually every business encounter. In fact, in today's world, the handshake is exchanged more frequently than currency. Most people have a pretty clear idea of what constitutes a good business handshake. No matter how many times I pose the question or how many people I ask in my presentations, I always get the same answer to the question, "What is the one word that describes a good business handshake?" Everyone says, "Firm." Yet saying it and doing it seem to be two different things. If you want to be impressive, be sure that "firm" describes the hand you extend and the grip you give.

It helps if you know the goal. What you are attempting to do is to make web-to-web contact with the other person's hand. Once the web of your hand meets the web of the other person's hand, close your thumb over the back of the person's hand and give a slight squeeze with your fingers. That's the critical point of the handshake. If there is no squeeze at the moment of contact, there is nothing firm about your grip. You have just handed the other person a "dead fish."

Be careful to avoid any handshakes that are seen or felt as inappropriate in business. Some people seem to think that a good handshake, particularly for a man, is one that causes pain. In fact, a bone-crushing grip sends a message that you are overbearing and insensitive.

Other handshakes to avoid in the work world are the "fingertip" and the "glove." Extending the tips of your fingers indicates a lack of confidence and uncertainty. Placing your left hand over the back of the other person's right hand constitutes the "glove" handshake that can be interpreted as too intimate or too controlling.

The handshake is more than just the grip. You need to make eye contact and smile at the other person. Step or lean into the handshake slightly, give two pumps of the arm from the elbow, not the shoulder (you are not pumping water at the well), and step back. Ever notice how some people won't let go? They just keeping on shaking and shaking. Business is not about holding hands, so remember to release the other person's hand after a pump or two. The good handshake should only last a few seconds, just long enough to make a great impression.

Being ready to shake hands wherever you are is important, but especially in business/social situations. When you are mixing and mingling at an after-hours event, keep your right hand free at all times. That means carrying plates and glasses in your left hand. This is not standard practice for most people, especially those who are right handed. Think how awkward it is to have someone extend a hand to you when you are holding a cold beverage in your right hand. There is that long uncomfortable delay while you switch the glass to your left hand. Then you try to figure out how to unobtrusively dry your cold, wet hand. Finally, after what seems like an eternity, you are ready to shake hands. The long pause can be avoided if you simply train yourself to hold items (plates, glasses, etc.) in your left hand.

The same rule applies in meetings and appointments. Always enter the room with items in your left hand. That includes papers, materials, briefcases and handbags. You never want to be caught fumbling around trying to free your hand, looking ill at ease and unprepared to extend your hand.

Let Me Introduce You

Introductions are invariably a part of business encounters. Whether you are in a situation where you need to introduce yourself or one where you have to introduce others, you'll want to do so with as much confidence and ease as you can muster. Once again, how you handle yourself is going to affect how other people judge you and whether or not you are perceived as professional. Next to table manners, people have more difficulty with introductions than any other aspect of good manners. Most people do not manage introductions well at all. They stutter and stammer while groping through the process. So if you want to set yourself apart from the crowd, put others at ease and make yourself look good, learn how to make introductions with skill and charm. Then practice what you have learned, and the next time you have to introduce someone, you will sail through the steps.

One of the most important introductions to make is of yourself. All too often, we fail to do this, perhaps assuming that the other person knows who we are or thinking that someone else will do it. It should go without saying that if you have never met a person before, you need to introduce yourself. Even though there are others around who know you, don't wait for someone else to take charge. Take the initiative to say who you are and to say something about yourself that will help the other person place you and facilitate a conversation.

There are also times when it is necessary to introduce yourself to someone you already know. Memorable as you think you are, it is quite possible that not everyone remembers you. Perhaps the person remembers your face, but not your name. How many times do you see people who look familiar, but you just can't come up with a name to go with the face? This works both ways. Don't put other people in the position of trying to guess who you are if there is any chance they may have forgotten you or your name. Walk up to people whom you haven't seen for a while or to people whom you may know from a completely different setting and give them the gift of your name. They will be grateful for your generosity.

Perhaps you can't remember the other person's name. Reintroducing yourself is a signal to that person to do the same. It works about eighty percent of the time. Every now and then you get a dud who doesn't understand the game and doesn't offer his name in return. Just be sure you are not the dud.

Now here comes the sticky part—handling introductions of other people and doing it well. Have you ever found yourself in a situation where it was obvious that some of the people didn't know each other, yet no one made an effort to introduce anyone? It was very awkward, wasn't it? Everyone notices when introductions aren't being made although no one says a word. This is clearly the time for you to step in, regardless of whether you know everyone or not, extend your hand and give your name. If you realize that people to whom you are talking don't know each other, take the responsibility for introducing them to each other. Host behavior will make you look confident.

Most often, people don't make introductions because they can't remember names. That is no excuse. Ignoring the introduction will only make it worse. If it happens to you, don't stall for time while you wait for some sort of divine intervention to give you the name. We only recall those things at three o'clock in the morning. So step up to the issue and confess that you have had a lapse of memory and ask forgiveness. Who hasn't forgotten a name and wouldn't be willing to forgive?

If you are reluctant to admit your shortcoming, try this technique. Say, "Do you two know each other?" There is an element of risk involved here, and it could backfire when these people look at you and reply, "No, we don't." At that point you are back to square one and forced to admit your deficiency.

There is a correct order to use in making introductions in business. You should always introduce a junior person or less important person (in title and position) to a senior or more important person. The way to do this is to say the name of the senior person first, followed by the words, "I'd like to introduce ___" or "I'd like to introduce to you ___." Then you give the name of the less senior person. You could say, "May I present ___," but that seems a bit stiff. Some people say, "This is ___," and while that is the least professional, it is acceptable and more comfortable for many people.

Be sure that you say something about each person you are introducing so that he or she will have a clue as to who the other person is and will have some information with which to start a conversation. Look at the person whose name you are saying while you make the introduction, and be generous in your comments. You'll look good, and the other people will feel good.

Introducing people to each other in business is a way to facilitate and establish relationships. Think about it, practice it, and take your time. You'll find yourself doing it with confidence and ease, no matter where you are or who is present.

I Never Can Remember Names

Are you guilty of having said this and of avoiding people because you forgot someone's name? You are not alone, but in business, remembering and using names is critical to your success. If you are going to move ahead, then you need to work on remembering names. The shelves are filled with books on how to improve your memory. The best I have found so far is *Remember Every Name Every Time* by Benjamin Levy. He uses the acronym FACE to aid in the process. FACE stands for focus, ask, comment and employ.

Focus on the other person the minute you meet. Make eye contact, smile and concentrate on the person's name and face. Most people are so busy thinking of what they are going to say next that they never even hear the other person's name.

Ask the person to repeat her name or repeat it yourself as if to clarify. For example, if the person says, "Hello, I'm Ginger," you simply ask, "Ginger?" The other person will appreciate your effort to be sure you have heard correctly, and you will be one step closer to fixing the name on your brain.

Comment on the name, either out loud or to yourself. You might say, "I like your name, Ginger. It reminds me of an dear friend." If the association is not one you think you should say out loud, say to yourself, "Oh, her name is Ginger, like the dog I had growing up."

Finally, employ the name. Use it in conversation immediately while you are still speaking with the person.

Your chances of remembering names will increase as you increase your efforts to remember.

Business Cards—Don't Leave the Office Without Them

Business cards are another aspect of those initial encounters with potential clients, employers or associates. The way you manage giving and receiving those cards will contribute to that critical first impression as well as your future relationship with clients or colleagues. The first step in this process of swapping business cards is to be sure that you have them with you at all times and that you are carrying a sufficient supply for the occasion. If you are conducting everyday business, you should have ten or fifteen cards with you. If you are attending a trade show, conference or traveling out of town, take a larger supply so you don't miss out on any opportunities to make lasting connections. I am always surprised when I met a businessperson who has to confess, "I just gave out my last card." I can't help but wonder how serious this person is about growing his business or furthering his career.

Keep your cards in a protective case so that they are always in mint condition when you pull them out. Nothing will take away from your professionalism as quickly as handing someone a dog-eared business card. Having a special card case that you keep in the same place in your jacket, briefcase or handbag assures that you can find your cards without having to fumble around awkwardly searching for them.

Women seem to have more of an issue with the search and fumble process. Women's jackets don't always have pockets where they can put business cards. A colleague of mine—Donna Fisher, author of *Power Networking*—recommends that business women have simple pockets sewn into the inside of their business suits for just this purpose.

Before you go to a business function, place a few cards in a your jacket pocket. Create a system for keeping your cards as well as the ones you collect during the event. If you are in the habit of carrying yours in your right-hand pocket, put the ones other people give you in your left-hand pocket. It can be embarrassing, to say the least, to hand out someone else's business card.

Know when and where to exchange your cards. As a rule, wait for the other person to ask for your card first. You hope that you have been so impressive that other people will want to have your contact information. If this doesn't happen, you certainly wouldn't want to miss a good business connection, so politely ask, "May I give you my card?" Or say, "May I have your card?" When you request someone's business card, that person will usually ask for yours in return.

When you meet someone who seems like good a connection, make sure that you get his card before you part company. If you need to write something on the card to remind yourself later who the person is and how or why you want to follow up, do it after he is out of sight. You never want to appear as if you are using the other person's valuable card as a piece of scratch paper.

By the same token, don't hand out cards that you have written on. If any of your contact information is no longer correct, get new cards printed. They are inexpensive and can be updated fairly quickly by most printers. With today's technology, many of us can produce quality pieces on our own.

The growing trend in some companies to have blank cards made up for each position in the organization (so that the current jobholder can fill in his/her name) conveys a message of instability and insecurity. It is a red flag signaling high turnover.

Since your business cards contain valuable information intended for special people, hand them out one at a time. When people offer up a handful at once, they devalue their cards as well as the people to whom they are being given.

Business cards are another step in the process of connecting with others in the world of work. The way you manage the exchange speaks to your professionalism.

Preparing for the Business Event

Woody Allen said, "Eighty percent of success is showing up." I would have to disagree. Simply showing up is not enough to guarantee your success at business functions, whether they are meetings, conferences, luncheons, banquets or cocktail receptions. How you handle yourself once you show up will determine how successful you are. And how successful you are at business/social events is directly proportional to the amount of preparation you put into attending the affair. There are some key questions you should ask yourself about each event before you go:

What is the purpose? Learn this before showing up for the event. Sometimes it is obvious by the invitation, which will state, for example, that a reception is being held to honor someone or to celebrate a particular occasion. If, however, the reason is not clear, ask someone. The most obvious choice to ask is the person responsible for sending out the invitations or the person who is handling replies. No one is ever offended by this kind of inquiry when it is normal and natural.

Who will be there? If you don't know who will be attending, find out. This is easy to do when you know who sent out the invitations. If they came from your organization, you should be able to get the guest list without difficulty. If another organization sent the invitations, call the person responsible and inquire about who else might be there. It is easy enough to explain that you are interested in knowing who the other attendees will be. Knowing whom you can expect to see will help you prepare what you will say.

What will I say? Knowing why the event is being held and who has been invited will help you determine the answer to this question. It may seem silly to suggest thinking about this ahead of time, but if you don't plan what you are going to say, you may find that you have nothing to say. The businessperson who can't carry on a conversation will have difficulty establishing and maintaining relationships.

Do your homework and get information on the people and organizations that will be represented. Read up on current affairs so you can carry on a conversation with anyone you meet.

What should you wear? This is a key question to consider. Too many people fail to verify the dress for the occasion and embarrass themselves by showing up in the wrong outfit. If the invitation does not specify the attire, call and ask. And always keep in mind that these events are about business and that your clothes should reflect your professionalism. It is better to err on the side of overdressing than underdressing.

Working the Event

To make the most of business/social functions, plan your arrival thoughtfully. If you arrive at the event five or ten minutes ahead of time, you will be in a position to meet the other guests as they arrive. By standing near the door, you'll be able to see people that you want to speak to as they arrive. A friend of mine who speaks on alliance building advises his clients to arrive ahead of time and to stand exactly fifteen feet inside the door, at a forty-five-degree angle. It's not necessary to carry a slide rule with you, but you get the point. Put yourself in a position to make the most of the occasion.

By not getting to the event within the first fifteen minutes, you will have difficulty finding the people you want to speak to in a crowded room, and you may have trouble getting into conversations with people who already have them well under way.

Another reason you want to be early is to avoid the crowd and get the lay of land. You are not there ahead of time so you can beat everyone else to the food. You didn't come to eat and drink. You're there to meet and greet, so do yourself a favor and eat or drink something before you go. That will take the edge off your appetite and leave you free to make personal connections.

A word of caution about arriving too early: If you arrive more than ten minutes early, be aware that you do run the risk of interfering with the last-minute preparations of your host.

Starting and Sustaining Conversation

Whatever the reason for the event, your purpose for being there is to establish new business relationships or nurture existing ones. You can only do this by interacting with others and engaging them in conversation.

The concept is easy, but the reality may be difficult. Talking to strangers is often challenging, especially since most of us grew up being told not to talk to strangers. Now suddenly, in the business world, we discover that to increase our contacts and to be more successful, we need to engage in conversation with people we've never spoken to before and perhaps never even seen before. Sometimes the person to whom we need to talk is not a total stranger. It could be someone you already know but not well enough to have ever had a conversation.

So how do you start a conversation? Back in the eighteenth century, the writer Samuel Johnson said, "Questioning is not the mode of conversation among gentlemen." That was then. This is now. If you want to start a conversation today, ask questions. Make sure you ask the right questions, though. Those are the open-ended ones or the ones that elicit more than a one-word response. If you walk up to someone and say, "Nice day, isn't it?" the probable reply is simply, "Yes." If, however, you ask, "What do you think of this nice weather?" you have increased your chances of getting a more interesting response.

Using the words, "why" and "how" instead of "what," "where" and "when" will elicit better responses. Another great technique is the one television interviewers use: "Tell me about ___." It is almost impossible to give a one-word answer to that statement.

Another way to start a conversation is to make a statement followed by a question. You might say, "This is a very well planned conference. What has been the best part of it for you so far?" You can also use a closed-ended question to warm things up and follow that with your open-ended question: "Isn't this a great conference? What is your favorite session so far?"

Once you've asked the first question and the other person responds, you can follow up with more questions based on the previous answer. It is the most effective way to build a conversation. People like to talk about themselves, so if you show an interest in what they are saying, they will keep talking.

Showing an interest in what the other person is saying requires basic listening skills. Here is a list of some ways to show you are tuned in:

1. **Pay attention**. Try not to think about what you are going to say next. Instead, focus on what the other person is saying so you can ask the next question based on that information.

2. **Nod your head occasionally** while the other person is speaking. That offers encouragement for the person to continue.

3. **Paraphrase what is being said**. By repeating in your own words a statement that the other person has just made, you verify that you are tuned in.

4. **Look the other person in the eye**. By maintaining eye contact, you show interest in what is being said, and you get clear signals about how the conversation is going from the other person's perspective. If his eyes glaze over or he starts looking around the room, it may be time to change the subject or move on.

5. **Let the other person finish speaking** before you jump in with your response. If someone hesitates only slightly in mid-sentence, many of us are tempted to complete the sentence or simply add our own. No matter how enlightening your next comment may be, the person who is interrupted will not be impressed. Pauses are good; interruptions are not.

6. **Smile**. That is the best way to let the other person know that you are enjoying the conversation. Of course, make sure that smiling is appropriate to the circumstances. If the

other person is describing his latest skiing accident, you may want to consider a different facial expression.

Being thoughtful about the kinds of questions that you ask and using good listening techniques will make you a good conversationalist and help you to establish those valuable business connections. However, don't leave anything to chance. Just as you prepared for the event by inquiring about the occasion and finding out who would be there, plan your conversation starters in advance. If you think that you can just show up and magically have meaningful conversations, you won't. When I attend business/social functions in my home city, I invariably encounter the same person at every event. He is the CEO of a major corporation. After I say, "Hello, how are you?" I am always stumped about what to say next. We just sort of stand and smile at each other. Then we say, "Well, good to see you," and we move on. After years of doing this, I finally figured out that I need to count on seeing this person and that I should plan what I am going to say to him (or rather, what I am going to *ask* him!).

Plan your conversation starters. Have a few questions that you can ask specific people you will see and other questions that you can ask anyone who shows up. Your questions may have to do with current events as long as they are not controversial. The weather is a safe topic, but it's generally overdone, so you need to work at keeping it interesting beyond, "Nice day, isn't it?" Make a list of the questions you can use to get others talking, and review them before you go to an event. If you wait until you are standing in front of someone and then try to come up with the winning question, it won't happen. Your mind will be a complete blank, and you'll end up saying something idiotic or nothing at all.

It is just as important to have conversation enders as well as conversation starters. The point of business/social functions is to interact with as many people as possible. Business people need to be as good as politicians at working the crowd. You will be wasting your time if you spend all of it talking to the same person. Even if you are enjoying the conversation, move on after a few minutes to someone else. It may be that you are not enjoying the conversation, but you find yourself stuck with one person. If you plan your exit lines ahead of time, you'll be able to extricate yourself from both pleasant and painful situations.

Whatever great exit line you have, use it after you have finished speaking. If you utter your farewell remarks as soon as the other person has stopped speaking, you will make her feel that you couldn't wait to get away. So let the other person finish and make a few comments yourself, quickly followed by your good-bye. Your exit line could be, "It's been very nice meeting you and talking to you, but someone has just come in that I need to speak with. Would you excuse me, please?" Or you could say, "It's been very nice meeting you and talking to you. I'd like to get something to eat. Would you excuse me, please?" If you'd like to follow up with people, let them know this. In your parting comments, say that you would like to call or go to lunch soon. Obviously, don't make that suggestion if you don't plan to follow through.

Sometimes we unwittingly kill conversation when we don't intend to. Here are some "killer" techniques to avoid:

1. **Interrogation**. Questions are the best way to start and sustain a conversation, but they can be overdone. Give people time to fully respond to what you have already asked, and make your next questions follow what you have heard. Firing one question after the other, particularly if they seem unrelated, will make the other person uncomfortable.

2. **Interruption**. If the person who is speaking stops long enough to draw breath, wait. Silence is not a bad thing. Be ready with your next question or comment, but don't jump in until you are sure the other person has finished.

3. **One-upmanship**. Don't we all have a better story to tell? One that can top what we just heard? I fell and broke my foot several years ago. Whenever I see someone with a cast on her foot, I recognize a great conversation starter; but I have to hold myself back from describing my accident, trying to outdo her story and killing the conversation.

4. **Advising**. When someone starts to describe an issue or a problem she is having, isn't it tempting to try to fix it for her? Most of us think we have answers to so many other people's problems. However, unless you are specifically asked for your advice, keep it to yourself. You may just kill the conversation when you begin to meddle.

In summary, if you want to be successful as a conversationalist, prepare for the event, practice what you will say, and pay attention to what others are saying. It is all about the other person. The best conversationalist in the world is the one who gets others to talk. If you can do that, you will be thought of as a fascinating person.

Think back to Robert and Barbara at the beginning of the chapter. Barbara knows that it is the details—those seemingly insignificant things like making eye contact, smiling at other people, saying someone's name in conversation, using the right tone of voice, focusing on other people and preparing for situations before they arise—that will contribute to her success. Barbara understands that manners do matter in the business world. She became aware early in her work life that the way she treated others would be important to how far and how fast she moved up the career ladder. She is clear that these behaviors have nothing to do with being stuffy, aloof and putting on airs but that they have everything to do with being courteous and respectful of other people.

If you want to be successful, remember three things:

1. **Pay attention to the fine points**. As J.W. Marriott said, "It's the little things that make the big things possible."
2. **Do your homework on the rules of etiquette**. Heed the admonition of Yogi Berra, who observed, "It's not the things we don't know that get us in trouble. It's the things we know for sure that just ain't so."
3. **Be authentic**. Incorporate good manners in all that you do so that they become part of you and define who you are, both personally and professionally.

Lydia Ramsey

Lydia Ramsey is the founder and president of Manners That Sell, a company that conducts presentations for organizations that want their employees to be at ease in any business situation and to represent them well in the marketplace. Lydia's light-hearted approach to business etiquette gives those who attend her workshops and read her publications the confidence and authority to build better relationships with clients, colleagues and coworkers. Her belief that business is based on relationships and that manners *DO* matter has helped organizations to attract and retain more clients and to increase their profits. Lydia is the author of *Manners That Sell: Adding The Polish That Builds Profits* and *Table Manners That Sell: 85 Tips For Dining For Success.* She is the co-author of *The Etiquette Of Networking: 99 Tips For Connecting With Courtesy.* She is a columnist for the Savannah Morning News and a contributing writer to numerous magazines, trade journals and online publications. She has been quoted or featured in The Wall Street Journal, The Los Angeles Times, Cosmopolitan and Woman's Day. Happy clients who sing her praises include corporations, associations, colleges and universities.

Lydia Ramsey
Manners That Sell
P.O. Box 16545
Savannah, GA 31416
(912) 598-9812, Office
(912) 598-0605, Fax
E-mail: Lydia@mannersthatsell.com
Web: www.mannersthatsell.com

Chapter 6

"So—What Do *You* Do?"
How to Respond With Your Head
and Your Heart!

Jan Dwyer

"So, what do *you* do?" the woman asked with a bored expression. She had asked this same question to a number of other guests at the party, but no one seemed to be the least bit interested in the answer— neither she nor the people she was asking! But this time the man answering her question had such excitement and eagerness in his voice that the woman couldn't help but be swept away by his reply. He was doing more than making polite conversation. Everything about him was truly involved in the response; his speech, his facial expression and his body language radiated enthusiasm. Something in what he said and— perhaps, more importantly—how he said it, convinced her that this person was different. He was living out his passion—and it showed.

What about you? Are you living your passion? If you are like most people, you have heard about this "passion thing" countless times, and possibly, you may have even said, "Nice concept for some, but it hasn't worked for me!" Just doing "the life thing" is hard enough; there are bills to be paid, children to be fed, a house to be kept clean and relationships to be maintained and nurtured. And let's face it—in today's economy, does it even make sense to pursue your passion? People are fortunate enough just to have jobs. Isn't it too much to ask that you actually like what you are doing? And let's say that you do find your passion. Can you support yourself? This chapter will address these questions with practical suggestions that may give you a different perspective on passion. Because it actually *is* possible and even feasible to be excited about how you spend your life!

Are people living their passion? Richard Leider and David A. Shapiro, authors of the book, *Repacking Your Bags: Lighten Your Load for the Rest of Your Life*, claim that this is not the case. "The vast majority of people endure their jobs because they see no other way to make a living...At the very least, most jobs force us into a rhythm of weekend leisure, Monday blues, Wednesday 'hump days,' Friday T.G.I. F. and regular paychecks. Our minds and bodies become so attuned to these rhythms that they become part of our internal clocks. We forget that there are other ways to spend time or save it to do the things and be with the people we love. We forget that there are other pathways that lead out of the wilderness, away from the rat race."

I have asked the question, "How many of you have found your passion?" to countless participants in training classes, from Boeing employees to workers in state and county governments. Rarely do I have more than one or two people raise their hands. As the title character in the classic movie, *Mr. Deeds Goes to Town*, remarks as he observes the elite of Washington, D.C., "People are funny here. They work so hard, they forget to live."

Those of you who didn't grow up dreaming of being in any particular profession may be able to relate to my journey in finding my passion. After graduating with a business degree with three areas of emphasis, I went to one of the largest aerospace companies in the area to work as a computer programmer. I figured that technical experience would be valuable, no matter what career I ended up doing. I learned the hard way; sitting in front of a computer eight hours a day was not motivating for me. I transferred from there to a financial position within the Hughes Corporation, but again, it didn't seem like a good fit.

In 1986, I endured the first of what would be four layoffs in my career, so I pursued my goal of obtaining an MBA—tuition dollars that turned out to be well spent. After graduating from the University of Chicago's Graduate School of Business, I decided that marketing would be a much better match with my people-oriented personality. But after a few months in a marketing research position at an amusement park, I was caught in another downsizing. So there I was, living in Southern California with my parents. I had an MBA but no job.

It was during that time that I started doing some serious soul-searching, really analyzing and assessing what I wanted to do with the rest of my life. With most of the jobs I'd had, I would come home each day exhausted and drained of energy. So I asked myself what *did* energize me. The answer was public speaking—being in front of groups and inspiring them!

By that time, I had been a member of Toastmasters International for years, but I didn't really think there was a job out there that would allow me to utilize those skills. (Toastmasters International is the leading movement devoted to making effective oral communication a worldwide reality through it's over 9,000 member clubs that help men and women develop communication and leadership skills.) As part of one of my layoff packages, I was able to use the services of Lee Hecht Harrison, one of the premier global career transition firms. After attending their seminar, talking to their counselor and going through numerous career development classes and resources (including Richard Bolles' book, *What Color is Your Parachute?*), I discovered that throughout my life there was a pattern of successes that had relied upon specific skills and interests. But it wasn't until I was sitting in a job search workshop that it suddenly hit me! I wanted to do what that career trainer was doing! And so began my transition into the field of training and speaking.

In 1995, I attended a session at the Toastmasters International convention, and when asked to jot down my dreams on an index card, I wrote, "I want to be a professional speaker." Shortly after that, I joined the National Speakers Association and was privileged to obtain a position as a training consultant at World Vision, a Christian, non-profit relief and development organization. This opportunity was a great fit for me, merging my passion for training and helping others with my own values.

After a restructuring at World Vision in 1998, I went to Weyerhaeuser, a forest products company, where I worked with a business that designed and delivered training programs in mill sites all across the country. After the training business closed down in 2000, I pursued my index card dream of owning my own speaking and training company, which today is located in Federal Way, Washington. (Incidentally, I now work as an adjunct trainer for Lee Hecht Harrison!).

My own determination, not to mention my involvement with the numerous associations and people (too many to name) who shared with me their support and advice, were important factors in my reaching my goal. As a Christian, I believe that God had a lot to do with it. Indeed, I would be remiss if I didn't mention the day I met a seventy-year-old man, whose prayer literally propelled my transition into a new career. I had met him in Long Beach, California, in the summer of 1993 while I was pursuing jobs in both the marketing and training fields. I was impressed with how he was living out his passion; he was going up to people on the beach and sharing with strangers about how much God loves them. He turned to me, looked into my face and asked, "How can I pray for you?" I replied that I was pursuing two kinds of jobs. I'll never forget him asking me, "What is it you really want to do?" What came out of my mouth immediately was, "Training!" And he proceeded to pray for me, right out there on the beach. It has been said that the "prayers of a righteous man are strong and effective," and I believe God honored this man's prayer.

I also know that my father played a key role during that time in my life. He saw me going after two types of jobs and encouraged me to focus on one career path, to devote my time, energy and investment to one pursuit. As soon as I discovered that I was more interested in training and speaking, I took his advice. Today, I am thankful that I did!

Some people associate the word "passion" with living a dream job. But passion isn't necessarily related to a career. As Cindy Pain, a career consultant with Lee Hecht Harrison, shares, "So many people think that passion is only job-related or judged worthy by societal standards for the times. We have to expand the definition of a passion to include a 'life passion.' Some people find that being a mother or a father is living their passion; others desire to be at work 8 hours a day in the same position with the same company and go home to their passion; others may want to work diligently creating a loving home or volunteering to enhance a cause. Living your passion is much broader than you think!" I agree with her. Your passion may work itself out differently than others' do, but the point is that you are living your life designed the way God created you to live it. As John C. Maxwell writes in his book, *The Success Journey*, "Everyone has a purpose for which we were created. Our responsibility—and our greatest joy—is to identify it."

The dictionary defines passion as, "an intense, driving, over-mastering feeling or conviction" or "a strong liking or desire for or devotion to some activity, object, or concept." I define passion as: "Living your life connecting your heart with your head." What do I mean by that? Have you ever heard someone lament that logically, a particular job or opportunity made sense, but that his heart wasn't in it? Statements such as, "This job only pays the bills" or "I need to hang onto this job until retirement" are indicators that there is not a lot of heart in that person's work. Of course, people who say this may have passions elsewhere in life, but isn't it unfortunate that people spend so much of their lives in jobs they hate? Or maybe you have been in a situation where your heart belonged to a new ambition but the idea never became a reality and no forward steps were taken toward the fulfillment of that goal.

People who live their passions have a pattern of leading "integrated" lives. No matter what opportunities they choose, they make intentional decisions, and the majority of their lives are devoted to using their talents in whatever arena or manner works for them. It is the kind of living that is not just heart-oriented but smart-oriented!

Classical musician Christopher Parkening discovered that his passion was using his music to glorify God. He writes, "I realize honestly that whatever talent or ability any of us has been given, it has been given to us by God, and we're responsible to be good stewards of that talent." Do you see yourself as a steward of what you have been given? This may be one of the most compelling reasons to pursue your passion. God designed you for a certain purpose. And He only made one of you.

In his book, *Search for Significance*, Robert S. McGee writes, "There has never been another person like you in the history of mankind, nor will there ever be. God has made you an original, one of a kind, really somebody!" Think about it—there is only one of you, with your particular set of talents, skills, interests and desires; only one of you who has had the experiences that you have had, met the people that you have met and gone through joy and sorrow like you have. You are dynamically unique from everyone else. And only you can influence and inspire others because of what you uniquely bring to the table. Whether you are a housewife, father, business executive or teacher, God desires you to use what He uniquely gave you!

Sometimes there are other reasons for pursuing a passion. In the movie, *The Rookie*, Dennis Quaid portrays a baseball player whose passion is to make it into the major leagues at an age when most players are long since retired. As a little boy, he had dreamed of being a professional baseball player. But life got in the way; Quaid's character got married, had a family and became a chemistry teacher and a coach of a high school baseball team. But with the encouragement of others, his baseball team in particular, he follows through on a pact he makes with the boys and starts pursuing his life-long dream, despite the tremendous sacrifices made by his family and himself. In one crucial scene, the character's wife realizes that their seven-year-old son is watching a father who, despite the obstacles, is striving to achieve his dreams. Both parents realize that the son will be greatly impacted by the fulfillment of the father's dream. He will grow up believing in his own dreams because of what his father has been able to accomplish.

It's amazing what happens when you start living in your passion. Your positive influence becomes an irresistible force in helping shape others! Many a training participant or audience member has come up to me and said, "It looks like you love what you are doing!" In fact, a recent participant in one of my career workshops said, "You are amazing – a living testament to the importance of following your passion." It's exciting to see that our lives can be a testimony to the power of dreams.

When counseling individuals in transition or facilitating training for groups, it is always exciting for me to see the lights go on in my clients' eyes as they describe certain career goals and aspirations that may have lain dormant for years, never given the opportunity to flourish. They start to see their job transitions as gifts and welcome the opportunity to do the kinds of self-assessment and career analyses that, for many people, help uncover new "hidden treasures." I have been encouraged by the many times I have facilitated the "What Matters Most" training by Franklin-Covey. The following is a sample of some ideas that participants have generated when they contemplated what they wanted to do with their lives:

- Visit my mom and dad more.
- Sing again.
- Have a large garden in which I could spend numerous hours.
- Quit working and dedicate my time to raising my children.
- Sail the world with family and friends.
- Build a home (with the love of my life) near the ocean, where our children and grandchildren would come.

How Do You Find Your Passion?

There are numerous books on the subject of finding your passion, but I have put together a few tools and suggestions that may be helpful to you. You'll also find a list of resources at the end of this chapter.

Read Richard Bolles' *What Color is Your Parachute?* It's an excellent place to begin your exploration of your passion. (The Library of Congress chose this book as one of the twenty-five books that have shaped readers' lives and is one of the seven essential popular business books). Richard Bolles has been in the career development industry for more than thirty years, and it is his assessments that personally helped me make the transition to my passion! His epilogue section, "How to Find Your Mission in Life," and Appendix A: The Flower Exercise in the 2002 and 2003 editions of the book are valuable resources related to discovering one's passion. The following two strategies are part of The Flower Exercise:

1. Analyze Your Top Ten Accomplishments

One of his assessment exercises includes analyzing your top ten achievements. After listing your top ten accomplishments (anything that you felt good about doing and were good at), you analyze the action verbs that enabled you to accomplish them. Invariably, these strengths become patterns or themes in your life. As you compare those skill sets or competencies with certain careers, you will see how you can apply them in a specific career. As Richard Bolles says, "The reason most people are unhappy in their jobs is because of the skills they aren't using."

2. Think About All the Elements that can Impact Your Job Satisfaction

Another helpful analysis is to assess all of the factors that can impact your job satisfaction. These include the people you work with, the culture, the commute, the amount of travel and the opportunities for advancement and benefits, to name a few. By getting a clear assessment of these aspects, you will be intentionally choosing a job that fits you. In the November 17, 1999 *Wall Street Journal* article, "What Job Candidates Really Want to Know: Will I have a Life?" writer Sue Shellenbarger says, "Increasingly, college recruits are concerned about other criteria in a job, besides just the work they will be doing." Ms. Shellenbarger quotes Sandro Franchi, director of U.S. recruiting and staffing for Eli Lilly: "Recruits want to know, 'How do people work together, how are people treated, and is the work environment friendly and supportive?'" The article cites a Price Waterhouse Coopers survey of 2,500 university students in eleven countries, fifty-seven percent of whom named "attaining balance between personal life and career" as their primary career goal. Indeed, as I have worked with hundreds of clients, the majority have shared that achieving work-life balance is one of their most important values.

Marsha Sinetar, in her book, *Do What You Love, The Money Will Follow*, encourages readers to ask themselves these questions when trying to find their life's purpose:

1. What is my real life's purpose? What do I want to have accomplished when I look back upon my life in old age?
2. How, specifically, would I have to think, speak and act in order to bring that purpose into being? What habits would I

need to cultivate, and what would I have to delete from my present life to live out my true purpose?

3. What activities (daily choices, attitudes, concrete accomplishments) would I do if I lived as if my purpose meant something to me?

4. How would I live on a day-to-day basis if I respected myself, others, and my life's purpose?

In his book, *The Success Journey,* **John Maxwell encourages us to define success for ourselves. He suggests these questions that can help us identify our purpose/passion:**

1. For what am I searching? (What sets your soul on fire?)

2. Why was I created? (Assess your unique mix of abilities, the resources available to you, your personal history and the opportunities around you.)

3. Do I believe in my potential? President Theodore Roosevelt said, "Do what you can with what you have, where you are."

Get to know your strengths and styles. The more you know who you are in your natural style, the better you will be able to find those settings in which you don't have to spend energy trying to be someone that you are not. I am certified in both the Birkman and DiSC profile behavioral tools, both of which help uncover who people are in different settings and what they need within an environment to be able to perform within their strengths. You would be amazed at what can happen when you are really clear about your natural style and motivational pattern. It's also amazing how this self-awareness not only helps you deal with other people (these assessments are great for intact work teams) but also provides crucial information about what kind of career, environment and people suit you best.

Listen to others. Sometimes we can get a feel for our strengths based on the number of times people see something in us. I have been to many a Toastmasters meeting where someone said, "You should think about doing this full time." I still remember the comments of others while I worked as part of the organization and development team at Weyerhaeuser: "Jan, I see you influencing more people by being out on your own. I see you being famous!" (That hasn't come true yet, but it certainly is a blessing to be used by God in many different industries and companies in my business!) Another colleague and friend left a message on my voice mail that I kept for months. She said, "Jan, there was a woman pastor at a church I visited, who totally reminded me of you!"

Indeed, there is "wisdom in many counselors," and sometimes other people see our potential when we may not.

Get encouragement! Establish a "dream team"—a group of people (not necessarily related to your profession) upon whom you can call for help. These should be people who love you, know you and can support you as you strive to discover and work/live in your passion. I feel blessed to have a large dream team that includes my mom, family, friends and fellow speakers and trainers. Encouragement from others goes a long way toward helping you achieve your goal. In *Strengthening Your Grip*, Charles R. Swindoll defines encouragement as "the act of inspiring others with renewed courage, spirit or hope. When we encourage others we spur them on, we stimulate and affirm them." William Barclay, in *The Letter to the Hebrews*, writes this about encouragement: "One of the highest of human duties is the duty of encouragement... It is easy to pour cold water on their enthusiasm; it is easy to discourage others. The world is full of discouragers..." We've all been encouraged by a well-timed word from a friend or family member. A dream team can provide this for you regularly as you pursue you passion!

Make your passion a top priority. Richard A. Leider and David A. Shapiro, authors of *Repacking Your Bags: Lighten Your Load for the Rest of Your Life*, believe that most of us, "keep adding things and responsibilities until we get to the point that we can't manage them anymore. It's the Packing Principle." They say the solution is to decide how much you're really willing to carry, and then decide what goes and what stays. "Ultimately, it comes down to a series of tradeoffs. What are you willing to trade in one area of your life to get what you want in another? Repacking becomes a matter of finding the right balance between the important priorities in your life."

Analyze what could be holding you back. Are you operating out of faith or fear? John Ortberg, in *If You Want to Walk on Water, You've Got to Get out of the Boat*, speaks of fear as he writes about Peter's willingness to walk on water. "The choice to grow is the choice for the constant recurrence of fear. You've got to get out of the boat a little every day... If you get out of the boat, you will face the wind and the storm out there. But you might as well know now there is no guarantee that life in the boat is going to be any safer."

Ortberg cites Eileen Guder, who wrote, "You can live on bland food so as to avoid an ulcer, drink no tea, coffee or other stimulants in the name of health, go to bed early, stay away from night life, avoid all controversial subjects so as never to give offense, mind your own business, avoid involvement in other people's problems, spend money only on necessities and save all you can. You can still break your neck in the bathtub, and it will serve you right." The author says that in the Bible there are 366 occurrences of the phrase, "Do not be afraid." I think this is telling us something!

Listen to your life! Parker J. Palmer, author of *Let Your Life Speak*, writes, "Is the life I am living the same as the life that wants to live in me?" Before you tell your life what you intend to do with it, listen for what it intends to do with you. How we are to listen to our lives is a question worth exploring... If we are willing to walk quietly into the woods and sit silently for an hour or two at the base of a tree, the creature we are waiting for may well emerge, and out of the corner of an eye we will catch a glimpse of the precious wildness we seek." So think about what you can do to allow the space in your life that will enable you to listen.

Enlist the listening ear of a friend, family member or spouse. Look for some who really knows you—and share your thoughts and feelings about your job and your interests. Sometimes, that person will notice you light up when discussing different activities. Those instances often reveal significant, underlying passions that may have been kept untapped.

Pray and seek counsel. As a person of faith, I believe in the power of prayer and the answers provided through other people, conversations, and opportunities. Seeking your minister, rabbi or spiritual mentor may be helpful to you as you strive to find your passion.

Open your mind to exploration and creativity as you seek your passion. As Denis Waitley says, "Your imagination is your preview of life's coming attractions." Not every passion is work-oriented; some people have found that their passion is being a mother or a father. For example, you may be like one of my friends who says, "I enjoy being a father; it is the most exciting thing in my life!" Although he works, it seems apparent to me that his role of a father brings more fulfillment to his soul than what he does in the workplace.

Once you have an idea of your passion, step out and try it. Suzie Jary, MSW, CSW, a career counselor and consultant with Career Transition for Dancers, a national not-for-profit organization for professional dancers changing careers, says, "Pace your way into passion. Stoke the fire and take actions. The more you do and get invested, the more the fire grows. It's inside you."

Once you are clear about your passion, you are in a position to start stepping out in faith and making your dream happen. But I know what you are thinking! You can't afford it. Or you've given up on your dream because you tried it years ago, and it didn't work. Or you are simply discouraged. Instead of a dream team around you, you have been cursed with a "mean team"—people who have discouraged you instead of supported you. The next section will address these issues.

"I can't afford it!"

If you think your current financial situation makes it difficult or impossible to quit your job and pursue your passion, I say this: There is more than one way to skin a cat (although my two cats don't necessarily like that statement!). Even if you are in a situation where you can't quit your full time job, could you be satisfied incorporating aspects of your passion into your life *after* work? A "survival job" is one that pays the bills while you continue looking for your dream job. You don't give up on your dream, and who knows? You may find a transitional job that will better equip you for your future!

"Will my passion pay my bills?"

The answer to this question depends a lot on what passion you want to pursue. You certainly have a lot of choices as you decide how to incorporate your passion in your life. Many of my colleagues in the speaking and training industry keep their day jobs as long as they can while they pursue their side businesses (their passions). At some point, they realize that their side jobs can sustain their income level, so they leave their day jobs to pursue their passions full time. Some people never quit their day jobs because they are content living their passions outside of work.

"I don't have time!"

Is your life weighed down too much to even start thinking about your purpose? Indeed, as Stephen Covey says in his "What Matters Most" training, "Most people spend more time planning their vacation than they do planning their life!" I realize that life has its seasons, obligations and responsibilities, but if we don't make time for this journey of purpose, there will never be time. What can you do to make time for the kind of self-reflection and exploration that the journey of finding your passion requires? Here are some thoughts:

Join an accountability group. Similar to a dream team, the purpose of this group is to offer not just support but accountability. In the career outplacement field, sometimes you'll find "work teams" who meet every week and share what has and hasn't worked in the previous week's job search. In the speaking industry, I have heard this group called a "mastermind group." The point is that these people are committed to the process, and they can help keep you on track with and remain accountable for the passions you want to pursue.

Share your dreams. Something very powerful happens when we start voicing our dreams and goals. According to Dr. Donald Smith's book, *Creating Understanding: A Handbook for Christian Communication Across Cultural Landscapes*, "By communicating—that is, acting out or speaking a position—a commitment to that position develops and increases." Watch out—the more you say something, the more firmly you believe it, and the more likely you will take action!

"This doesn't work - I tried it before!"

When I give counsel to those in job loss situations, I tell them that their biggest asset is their self-esteem. In a job search—which is basically a "rejection journey"—how you feel about yourself, your confidence in yourself and in God (or whatever higher power you believe in) is crucial. Our beliefs may be as small as the mustard seed. And in times of intense suffering, trials and overwhelming circumstances, it is easy to doubt, to wonder, to ask God "Why?" and to allow all those emotions to overpower us.

If you talk with anyone who has achieved success, you'll probably learn that his or her journey had its share of rocky times. More than likely, your journey toward your dream or passion is likewise not a straight line to the top. There may be situations where it takes every ounce of strength and belief to continue on the road that you began. Being an entrepreneur in an industry filled with constraining budgets, downsizing workforces and shifting priorities has been a struggle for me! Many times, I would like to quit, and even as I write this chapter on passion, I wonder about my future. It hasn't been an easy road this last year. But I also know that there are ebbs and flows (sometimes more ebbs than flows), and I'm hanging on and climbing until I get a clear calling to do something else.

Eric Alexander also knows a lot about climbing. This world-class skier, climber and mountaineer defied all odds by scaling Mt. Everest with his blind friend, Eric Weihenmayer, whose goal was to summit the highest point on each of the seven continents. Climbing certainly wasn't a smooth, upward path. In September 2000, Alexander survived a near-fatal fall in the Himalayas while attempting to summit Ama Dablam. He fell 150 feet, landing on a three-foot ledge.

His organization, Adventure Beyond Limits, is dedicated to helping those with disabilities achieve their dreams. In a recent talk to the singles group at my church, Eric said, "I love to climb mountains. I always have. I believe God put this desire in my heart, and this passion is just screaming to get out. I have to do what I'm called to do." It reminds me of the scene from *The Rookie*, when the father of Dennis Quaid's character talks to his son about his dream. "Sometimes in life, it's not what you have to do but what you were meant to do." Despite the sacrifice, hard work and, yes, even danger, it is worth it to fulfill your dream and passion.

"I figured out my passion years ago. Why aren't I feeling fulfilled?"

We all change, so it makes sense that our passions change, too! A year ago, I began a medical journey wherein for months I didn't know if there was something wrong with me—all because of a questionable blood test. It was a rather scary time as I went from doctor to doctor, allowing my imagination to run wild with the implications of those lab results. Yet the journey enabled me to reassess what I was doing and ask myself, "If I died today, what would I regret not doing?" The answer was clear. I always had a calling to go to seminary, and despite the finances and travel distance and impact on my business, I pursued this dream. I am happy to report that the latest doctor's report came out negative and that I have now taken seven seminary classes!

"Can different passions be contradictory?"

Absolutely. I am probably living my own life with a few contradictions! I'm pursuing seminary, traveling five hours back and forth to classes every Monday, while trying to support myself in my business. That is why it is important to really listen and make sure that you make the main thing just that—the main thing. If you find yourself becoming emotionally and spiritually drained because you are too busy, this is a good indication that you may need to reassess your original dreams and see if you need to make adjustments in your schedule or time so you can live your passion.

In *Who Dares Wins*, author Peter Legge defines success: "Unless you have balance in your life, you can't be truly successful. If you have all the money in the world and no one likes you, wants to marry you or be with you, you aren't successful. Similarly, if you have a happy marriage and a comfortable home but can't sleep because you can't make the mortgage payments, you are out of balance. Pursue a worthy ideal, and keep your life in balance. That's success!"

We've talked about passion—what it is, how to find it—as well as some tips for moving through your journey. Have some of your viewpoints on this whole "passion thing" changed after reading this chapter? Living in your passion with your head and heart integrated and living your life as a good steward of the talents you have been given are some of the greatest gifts we have been given. Certainly your life is worth more than a two-week vacation, so spend some time away from the noise of life and reflect and plan on your life goals and dreams. The sheer act of doing some self-reflection will invariably help you to move in the direction of life that nurtures your soul. Your passion may be any number of pursuits, but it is important to be clear on what, exactly, you're pursuing. As Ralph Waldo Emerson said, "The world makes way for the person who knows where he or she is going." Or consider the words of William Wallace in the movie *Braveheart*: "We all die. Not everybody truly lives."

References

Bolles, Richard N. *What Color is Your Parachute?* Ten Speed Press, 2002.

Elsheimer, Janice. *The Creative Call*, Shaw Books, 2001.

Ortberg, John. *If You Want to Walk On Water, You've Got to Get out of the Boat*, Zondervan Publishing House, 2001.

Legge, Peter. *If Only I'd Said That (A Collection of Thoughts, Quotes and Words of Inspiration)*, Eaglet Publishing, 1999.

Legge, Peter. *Who Dares Wins*, Eaglet Publishing, 2001.

Leider, Richard J. and David A. Shapiro. *Repacking Your Bags: Lighten Your Load for the Rest of Your Life*, Berrett-Koehler Publishers, 1995.

Maxwell, John C. *The Success Journey: The Process of Living Your Dreams*, Maxwell Motivation, Inc., 1997.

McGee, Robert S. The Search for Significance, Rapha Publishing, 1990.

Miller, Arthur F. *The Power of Uniqueness*, Zondervan,1999.

Palmer, Parker J. *Let Your Life Speak: Listening to the Voice of Vocation*, Jossey-Bass, 2000.

Sinetar, Marsha. *Do What You Love, The Money Will Follow: Discovering Your Right Livelihood*, Dell Publishing, 1987.

Smith, Donald. *Creating Understanding: A Handbook for Christian Communication Across Cultural Landscapes*, Zondervan Publishing House, 1992.

Swindoll, Charles R. *Strengthening Your Grip*, Word Publishing, 1982.

Conferences and Presentations

Messages at the International Career Development Conference, The 19th Annual California Career Conference, November 2002

Messages at the Prevailing Church Conference, Willow Creek Church, May 2002

Jan Dwyer

Jan Dwyer empowers individuals, teams and companies to achieve results, build customers and create success. For over a decade, she has inspired audiences all over the country, delivering training sessions and keynotes for a broad array of audiences and industries. Jan partners with her clients by providing customized solutions that equip them with the ability to personally achieve their goals. With a University of Chicago MBA, and with hands-on experience in small business, non-profit, and Fortune 500 companies, Jan brings expertise that is grounded with easy-to-implement strategies. She is an in-demand speaker at a wide range of associations, conferences and church events. Jan's topics span customer service, career development, leadership, speaking and facilitation skills training, and communication skills. Her training and teambuilding sessions incorporate a wide variety of popular assessment instruments, including The Birkman and DiSC profiles. Jan is also a preferred provider of training and consulting services for the State of Washington. Her clients range from The Boeing Company, Weyerhaeuser Company, American Bible Society, Getty Images, Medtronic Physio-Control, Starbucks and Los Angeles County. She has been an active member of the National Speakers Association since 1995.

Jan Dwyer, MBA
Jan Dwyer & Associates
P.O. Box 23688
Federal Way, WA 98093
(253) 838-5880, Office
(253) 838-2522, Fax
Email: JanDwyer@aol.com
www.jandwyer.com

Chapter 7

The Changing World of Work

Dr. Cheryl Leitschuh, Ed.D. LP

Do you find that your organization is constantly changing—that you are not sure what organization you are working for, let alone your job description?

Has your job changed as a result of downsizing, outsizing and rightsizing, leaving you with more to do and less time?

Do you find that you struggle to put your life in balance and that work occupies a disproportionate amount of time in your life?

Do you ask yourself, "Am I in the right job?"

If you answer "yes" to any of these questions, you are not alone. The world of work is changing and becoming more demanding. You need to change with it. But how?

In my work as a coach, trainer and consultant, I have observed the changes in the world of work and the impact on the individual's stress, satisfaction and productivity. In the 1980s, organizations focused on quality. It was about doing the best for customers and providing quality products and services. The 1990s moved us into an era of speed. We were asked to do more, faster.

The facts are, however, that faster would be possible if organizations were not in constant change but that change will be a fact of life in the 21st century. We see very conservative industries like banking and phone companies merging and changing, often leaving employees struggling to remember the name of their employer. Research shows that the secret to dealing with constant speed and change is knowing who you are, your natural talents, what you desire and how to connect with the new changes.

This chapter will identify the components for establishing the solid foundation of information necessary to address the needs of the changing world of work. It will identify the paradigm for employees in the 21st century based on the leadership and management issues of the future. It will clarify the choices each individual needs to make. And finally, it will provide a step-by-step process to clarify your own vision and direction for the future.

The Work Paradigm Shifts

The changes in the world of work haven't just been observed in the course of my work; these changes have also been written about in leadership and management publications.

Peter Drucker has been the organizational and leadership expert since the 1950s. His early works indicated that the success for organizations was in establishing an efficient organizational structure and then hiring individuals to meet the needs of the structure. This made life much simpler for employees as they were clear on job expectations and how they operated within the organizational structure.

In Drucker's current book, *Management Challenges for the 21st Century* (HarperCollins, May 1999), he acknowledges that the old paradigm no longer works. Due to the realities of the marketplace, organizations need to be fluid in their structures and ready to reorganize to meet their own economic needs. He indicates that success for future organizations is in having flexible employees who are ready to change as the needs of the organization changes. Drucker states, "Success in the knowledge economy comes to those who know themselves—their strengths, their values and how they best perform." The old paradigm no longer works. A new paradigm is critical to the success of organizations in the 21st century. This paradigm requires that all workers be aware of their vision, the best role they play in achieving productivity and success. Additionally, each organization needs to understand the talents of its players and assign them to the most effective roles possible.

Organizations who have moved to this new paradigm are also seeing the economic results of making this shift. In the article, "Happy Workers, High Returns" (Jan. 12, 1998, p. 81), *Fortune* magazine looked at the 100 best companies to work for in America. The research for this article focused on the question, "Do happy workers improve corporate performance?" To obtain the answer, The Gallup organization surveyed 55,000 workers in an attempt to match employee attitudes with company results. The survey found that four attitudes, taken together, correlate strongly with higher company profits. The four attitudes are:

1. Workers feel they are given the opportunity to do what they do best every day.
2. They believe their opinions counts
3. They sense that their fellow workers are committed to quality.
4. They have made a direct connection between their work and the company's mission.

A New Paradigm—A New Dilemma

This new paradigm creates an interesting dilemma. Most individual employees have not been taught how to create visions for their careers. Most employees cannot clearly identify the best roles they play in the work world using their talents and abilities. In my speaking and training, I ask groups if they learned how to create a career vision, or focus, in high school. Few, if any, hands go up. In college? Maybe a couple more hands go up. The largest response comes when I ask how many have taken the time to search the answers to these questions themselves. Most of us have never learned how to create visions for ourselves, how to operate from a sense of our strengths and bring our strengths to our work world at every endeavor. It's not difficult, but it does take time and an understanding of the factors necessary to create a clear and complete vision.

The mission of my organization has been to be a resource to both individuals and organizations in answering these questions. As we have developed the tools, both individuals and organizations have benefited. My goal is to assist workers and organizations in understanding the dynamics that are necessary in addressing the needs of the changing world of work. The benefit for the organization is increased productivity, retention and bottom-line results. The benefits for the individual are reduced stress along with greater balance, purpose and direction.

The Realities of Employees Being Human

While we can change many things, we cannot change the essence of human nature. As humans, we have an innate stress response that occurs when any demand is placed upon us. We are designed to deal with the stressor but need time to recover before the next stress occurs. Most of us have very few days when we deal with only one stress and have ample time to recover. The reality is that we live in a world of chronic stress. Change creates this stress. Change always produces stress whether it is positive or negative. If we respond to all these requests and challenges without choosing, it inevitably leads us to a level of burnout and a level of unbalance that is not healthy.

In order to accept the realities of being human and dealing with the ever-present stress response, we need to consciously choose how we focus our attention. If we do not make this choice, we end up in the stress cycle. If we do make the choice, we can operate from the balanced cycle. The stress cycle leads to burnout, depression and physical challenges. The balanced cycle leads to success, satisfaction and direction.

When we are in the stress cycle, we operate from short-term solutions. Imagine a bull's eye, a fixed target that absorbs the impact of everything hurled its way. It's no wonder that we experience physical, emotional and mental symptoms when we literally become the targets of all the requests that come at us from the outside world.

When we operate from the balanced cycle, we operate with a sense of focus, of longer-term thinking. We operate with a sense of knowing what we are looking for and base choices on this grounded information. Instead of a target, think of a baseball catcher. We catch the requests and decide what to do based on a set of criteria or data. In order to achieve this point of grounding and balance, we need to understand who we are, our natural talents, our values. It can't be someone else's talents and values or we bounce back to the stress cycle. No one else is an expert on who you are and what you want. Only you can provide the content, given the right process.

The New Paradigm

The remainder of this chapter is designed as a road map to address what people need to do to move forward in the changing world of work. Some readers will find they are able to work with the factors and develop the tools independently. Others may find the need for a coach or mentor to process the information in order to ensure the best possible perspective and integration of the material. Whatever way is chosen, the content is designed to give a clear understanding of the process and reflection needed to shift to the success paradigm of the 21st century.

Eight factors needed to build the foundation of this paradigm:
1. Career Development Cycle
2. Abilities
3. Skills
4. Interests
5. Personal Style
6. Family Beliefs
7. Values
8. Goals

Career Development Cycle

There are two areas to consider in the career development cycle. First is identifying whether you are in a building or transition stage in your career. Second is gathering the wisdom from past experiences (and there is wisdom) to ask better questions for the future.

It is normal to go through periods of your life when you ask, "Is this all there is? What's the next step? What do I want to do for the rest of my life?" Mid-life crisis is identified as one of these points. However, in this fast-paced world of speed and change, these questions may be triggered by changes in your environment. It might be from layoffs, technology or job reassignments. When these questions begin, your level of success does not stop the process. Success does not bring immunity to transitions.

The greatest resources for identifying your stage in the career development cycle are Gayle Sheehy's books *New Passages* and *Understanding Men's Passages*, in which the author differentiates between life-building stages and transition points. Building stages are times when you feel that you are in the right fit for your career and life. Energy, excitement, curiosity and happiness come from being in the right place. Then the transition occurs, and anxiety, depression, uncertainty and low self-confidence take over.

Which would you prefer? Would you rather be in a position of excitement, energy and happiness? Or would you rather be in a point of depression, uncertainty and low self-esteem? Most people would say they would rather be experiencing the excitement rather than the depression.

If people move too quickly from uncertain emotions to try to get to the happiness, they often make emotional decisions instead of wise decisions. Wise decisions come from evaluating what is needed and operating from a set of criteria instead of subjective emotions. During the emotional state of mind, impulsivity and anxiety cause people to move quickly to decrease the stress. Typically what happens is a boomerang back to that the uncertainly as the decision was not based on wisdom, only emotion.

By creating a personal vision, decisions are made from the wise mind as it creates the road map to manage the emotional mind. It is always easier to work on creating a vision when you are in the building stage. However, the majority of individuals I work with do not realize the importance of a vision until they are in a transition point. Managing the emotions is a critical component of creating a vision while in transition. A neutral perspective, such as that offered by a coach, will be a necessary ingredient to create a vision of the wisdom.

Understand where you are right now. What do you need to operate from your wise mind? How can you manage the emotions of a transition time in order to operate from your wise mind?

The second area of career development is to explore the wisdom you have from the past to ask better questions for the future. The easiest way to identify this wisdom is to first draw a career time line, starting with the first job you ever had, even if it was a lemonade stand at the age of five. Draw a spot on the line that represents each of your jobs, whether paid or unpaid.

Now answer the following questions at each point along the line:
1. What did you like?
2. What did you hate?
3. What skills did you use in each job?

When you are finished, look for patterns or wisdoms that can direct you to future choices. Document the observations in one of three ways: validating information, information forgotten or new awareness never observed before.

Abilities

Abilities are different than skills. Abilities are what come natural and easy to you. Research shows that abilities can be measured by age fourteen and do not change throughout your lifetime (The Highlands Program, 1986). Think of abilities as the hardware for your human computer.

There are a few ways to understand your abilities. One is to review the career time line again. This time, identify the times you were operating on autopilot—the times when work seemed effortless and your satisfaction level was at its highest. What kinds of activities were you doing? This may indicate that you were operating from your core talents or abilities.

The Highlands Ability Battery is a very useful assessment that can help you better understand these core talents and abilities. It uses timed work samples to have the individual show her natural abilities. This is very different from self-report assessments that ask, "Do you like trees or water? Color in the correct circle." In the self-report assessment, the individual identifies what she *believes* to be true. In a true ability assessment, the individual shows her natural abilities without bias. For additional information about this assessment, visit our web site at www.career-future.com.

Skills

Skills are the things that you have learned. They are the software that is guided by the hardware (your abilities). We've all learned many things, some of which we enjoy doing and some of which we don't. For instance, I have learned accounting skills, but I would quickly become a performance problem if I were asked to deliver accounting skills on a regular basis. It's important to take a look at your skills to understand the ones that are transferable to other kinds of positions. What skills do you want to continue to use? What skills do you have but have no desire to use?

Let me provide an example of the difference between skills and abilities. I have had the opportunity to work with psychology interns in the course of my job. I might have two interns from the same school, with the same GPA. One of the interns will need a lot of information to determine the cause of an issue or problem. He will prefer working with checklists and need time for careful consideration of the facts to determine a psychological need. The second intern will be able to quickly assess the issue without formalized process or detailed information. Will one be a better psychologist than the other? Both have the same training and skills. The difference may be the ability set. The software is the same, but the hardware is different. Both may be wonderful psychologists, but the role and environments in which they work will need to be consistent with their ability sets. If we place the individual needing the time to assess the issues into an emergency room environment, he will probably experience a lot of distress. He may even conclude that he is not designed to be a psychologist. This would be an inaccurate conclusion. Psychology may not be the issue; it may be the work role and environment.

Do you see the difference? Many individuals are not in the wrong field or profession but are mismatched in their work roles or environments because they do not understand their natural abilities. Your current occupation may not be the problem; how you deliver the results may be the challenge. Understanding your abilities and your skills may lead to understanding the mismatch.

Interests

Interests are the things that bring passion and enjoyment to your life. These are the things that only you can know about. They might be things that you can integrate into your career and work world, or they may be activities that can only happen in your outside world but need to happen in order for you to have a sense of balance and excitement about life.

Let me provide you with an example. I work with a woman who was in a management-level position. She was out of balance, extremely stressed, looking at leaving her position but unsure where to go. When we began talking about areas of interest, she identified needlepoint as something she loved. You could see the softening of her expression as she began to talk about needlepoint. When I asked her how she integrated needlepoint into her life at that time, she sheepishly stated that she had put her needlepoint in the closet when she took on her new management position. She was afraid that the time required for this new position would not leave time for needlepoint.

That was four years ago. At the time, I encouraged her to take the needlepoint back out of the closet and begin to integrate this area of interest into her daily life. The needlepoint gave her time to think and brought peace back into her life. This had a tremendous impact on decisions she made related to her career. She did not leave her organization or her position. She was able to tailor the position, delegate some additional responsibilities to others and negotiate the day-to-day responsibilities with her supervisor. I attribute all of that to her being able to put balance back into her life by adding a necessary ingredient—the needlepoint. No one could know this—only her. It seemed so simple yet so crucial to her balance, peace and focus.

What are your interests? Is it golf? Is it reading? Are there things you could integrate into your work world? Perhaps it is not something you can bring to your work but an ingredient that is necessary in your personal life. Whatever it is, it is uniquely yours. Use it. Don't neglect your interests. They may be a critical element for success, balance and fulfillment.

Personal style

Personality is very different than abilities. Personal style is the flavor, the spice that you add to the vision. You may have completed inventories such as the Myers-Briggs or the DiSC profile. If you have never completed a personal style assessment, I recommend you visit the Internet site www.advisorteam.com. By using this type of information, you can gain insight into what you need daily within your world of work: the kind of environment, interaction with people, time by yourself, types of problems and information to solve problems. This depth of information will be a necessary component for the final process.

Family Beliefs

When we talk about family, we talk about the beliefs that our families have instilled in us that relate to success and work. What does success and work mean in your family?

It is a very different world of work than it was in our parent's time, but those beliefs still continue to impact us. Here is an example: I was working with an individual who grew up on a farm, something that is quite prevalent here in the Midwest. One of the messages he learned from his family was that work is a twenty-four-hour-a-day, seven-day-a-week proposition. He not only grew up on a farm but on a dairy farm, and the challenge with dairy farming is that you are constantly on duty. You can't take a day off. You can't say to the cows, "I'll milk you tomorrow—I have other things to do," because your entire livelihood is on the line.

When this gentleman looked at his family beliefs about work and success, he began to realize that this message was alive and well in his life. He was working twenty-four hours a day, seven days a week and believed that success was a very fragile thing. Interestingly, he was not farming—he was selling insurance. He began to realize that working twenty-four/seven had cost him relationships. He was on his third marriage. His children were not speaking to him. He was frustrated with his job because it was all consuming. There was no time in his life for enjoyment and satisfaction. By shifting some of his work beliefs, he was able to give himself permission to have time for relationships, balance and satisfaction.

What beliefs about success do you have? Different generations have different beliefs about success. The beliefs of your parents may not be the beliefs that are going to lead you to success. On the other hand, the beliefs that your parents had about success and work may be exactly what you need to be successful. Only through the awareness of these beliefs can you understand, change or modify them to become more consistent with your desired future direction.

Here is an exercise:

- Interview your parents, or someone close to your parents, and ask the following questions:
  1. What was success for you?
  2. How did you choose your career?
  3. Were there changes you made in your career to achieve greater success, satisfaction or direction?
- Answer these same questions for yourself.
- Compare the answers to identify the patterns of beliefs.
- Decide what beliefs will be useful to your future success, satisfaction and fulfillment.

Values

Values are the guiding principles that bring meaning and focus to our lives. Understanding your values and how you choose to live your values is a key element of the vision.

Let's do a value exercise. Take a look at the following list of values:
1. Pleasure
2. High earnings
3. Helping society
4. Wisdom
5. Health
6. Risk-taking
7. Friendship
8. Competence
9. Sense of accomplishment
10. Creative expression
11. Spirituality
12. Leadership
13. Affiliation
14. Family

Rank these values in order, from one to fourteen, with one representing the most important value and fourteen the least important.

This exercise should force you to make some choices. No one in the world can dictate your values. Only you can understand and identify these key guiding principles for your life.

Now take this same set of values, but rank the values based on where you have spent your time in the last week, number one representing where you have spent the most time and fourteen representing the area on which you spent the least amount of time.

The first list identifies what is most important. The second list gives a reality check of whether you are living a life consistent with what you say is important. Are you saying one thing and doing another? Inconsistency can be one of the greatest areas of stress.

Sometimes life gives you the choice to spend time in ways that contrast with your values. But the key word here is "choose." Are you choosing, or are situations choosing your life direction for you? Take a look at the two lists. Identify any disconnects or choices you need to make.

Goals

Goals are what you want to achieve in your life. What is important to you? What do you want to happen in your life, in your career, in your family? I encourage you to write down everything possible you can think of. Don't screen anything out. Just make the list. We'll worry about when, where and how later on.

As adults, we often screen the goals before we identify the goals. Questions arise such as, "Can I achieve this goal?" With the changing world of work, many things become possible that may seem impossible at this point in time. By screening before identifying the goals, you eliminate the doors that could possibly open for you in the future.

Take a clean sheet of paper and begin to write down every dream you have ever had. No screening is allowed. Keep this foundation piece for the next step in the process, the vision portfolio.

Putting the Pieces Together

Once you have gathered the material for the eight foundations of your new paradigm, there are three steps needed to complete the process.
1. Vision Portfolio
2. Vision Statement
3. Action Plan

The Vision Portfolio

If you have completed the exercises above, you have the data to start your vision portfolio. What is a vision portfolio? Think of it as the stir-fry pan in which you mix together the ingredients you have worked so hard to prepare.

Chose a notebook, binder or file to compile the contents of your portfolio. Provide a separate section for each of the foundational areas and gather the information relevant to each section. It may be information from previous assessments or new information from this chapter. The important thing is to gather the information in one location.

As you assemble the material, you may realize the need for additional information in one of the foundational sections. If so, targeting specific books or assessments might be useful. Here is where the use of a coach can be extremely important. It is important to ensure that you have the critical information you need to make a wise-mind decision.

The Vision Statement

The next step is the vision statement. For this, you will need to set up two additional sections in your notebook or file:
1. What I Intend to Create with My Life
2. What I Intend to Create with My Career

Steps for the vision statement exercise:

- On one sheet of paper, write "What I Intend to Create with My Life" at the top of the page. On a second sheet, write "What I Intend to Create with My Career" at the top.
- Go back to each section of the portfolio and list or bullet key elements you believe are necessary to complete the criteria for each of the statements.

Many people feel that what they are writing is obvious. Obvious? Maybe. But keeping the data in your head limits the usefulness of your vision. Write it down, put it in the stir-fry, and observe what it says to you.

Once you have completed this part of the exercise, you are now ready to write your first vision statements—one for your life and one for your career. If you have written a previous vision statement, bring it out and rewrite it to include this new information. WARNING! Some people get stuck here. They aren't sure what to write or how it should look. "Will it be correct? Will other people laugh?" Don't worry about any of this. Whatever you write will be perfect. It will be yours, based on your data.

The process may feel uncomfortable. This is probably the first time you have written a vision statement based on objective data. Expect some discomfort. It will become more comfortable as you live with it, play with it and dance with it. Yes, dance with it. It should bring a sense of joy and excitement strong enough to make you want to dance. Over time, it will be worked and reworked as you add additional insights and information. The key is to start with what you have now. You can enhance and polish as you move forward with your life.

Your Action Plan

A vision without action is merely a dream. Your new paradigm should include clear action steps that result in movement toward the success you desire. In order to understand how the Action Plan process works, let me share with you two clients experiences which are fairly typical of the majority of clients I see.

When Anita began the Career Vision process, she was unsure of her direction within her company. Her questions were "Am I in the right career fit?" and "What should I do to move forward in my career?" Her company saw the wisdom of helping her to answer these questions and sent her into this process. After completing the Career Vision process, Anita was able to compare her current position with her vision. Her conclusion was that she was indeed on track but needed to make some steps to improve her satisfaction and consistency between her vision, talents and current career position. Her action plan included the following steps:

1. Discuss with her supervisor the results of this process.
2. Redesign the work tasks within her department to allow her more time to focus on her natural talents and abilities.
3. Target specific training programs to enhance her skills.
4. Begin more consistent daily time management practices to remain consistent with her priority of putting family first in her life.
5. Share with her team ways that they could better communicate with her and she with them.

This example shows how the visioning process may lead you to see that your vision is very consistent with what you are already doing. Don't be surprised if this happens. The majority of people do find that they are moving in the right direction. All they need is a five- to ten-degree change in how they design their day, their job, etc. The action plan may focus on these incremental movements. Think back to geometry class and the impact that a five- to ten-degree change can have over time. We make the mistake of thinking that visions need to be life-changing. Sometimes visions simply offer the baby steps needed to get us back on track.

The second example is of a client named Roger. He came to the Career Vision program clearly miserable with what he was doing. While he was able to perform his job, the distress he felt on a daily basis was taking a huge toll on his physical, mental and emotional well-being. The visioning process provided a criteria list of what he needed to be satisfied, motivated and productive in his career. In comparing that to his current position, it became very clear as to why he was experiencing significant distress. Once he knew why, it was time to take action. His action plan included the following:

1. Create a networking document to assist in sharing with others the type of position he was looking for.
2. Create a list of 100 networking names with which to share this document.
3. Set a goal of 10 names per week to contact.
4. Share with his supervisor and HR his desire for a different position and the criteria for greater satisfaction, motivation and productivity.

If your vision does move you in a new direction, you can now move with clarity of focus. Wouldn't it be wonderful if you could wave the magic wand and make it happen in an instant? Often we need to take steps to move in the new direction. The key is knowing which direction to move and what steps to take. This action plan will focus on the steps needed to make this movement toward a vision that will become reality. The vision guides the action, but without action we merely have a dream.

Moving Forward

"(We) will have to learn to manage ourselves. We will have to learn to develop ourselves. We will have to place ourselves where we can make the greatest contribution. And we will have to stay alert and engaged during a fifty-year working life, which means knowing how and when to change the work we do." (Drucker, Management Challenges of the 21st Century, 1999)

We all know that the world of work is changing. If our heads don't tell us this, our emotions certainly do. This new world of work creates the opportunity and challenge to learn a new way to see yourself as the tool that brings success. It also brings the challenge of knowing what to do to become proactive in dealing with these changes. Creating awareness through an objective vision and intentional action plan will be the road map into the 21st century work world.

Dr. Cheryl Leitschuh, Ed.D. LP

Dr. Cheryl Leitschuh, Ed.D. assists companies in achieving their key business objectives by fully capitalizing on a single line of their balance sheet - their human resource potential. Cheryl uses powerful programming, assessments and technology to harness and then maximize the untapped potential of a company's human resource assets. When working with individuals, her typical engagements include developing key leaders and managers, enhancing talent development, developing focus in vision and implementing this vision both personally and professionally. When working with an organization, Dr. Leitschuh addresses the short term and long term business objectives by focusing on human talent development. These projects have focused on conflict resolution, trust management and enhancing team performance. Cheryl has a broad range of clients that include health care, high tech and professional service firms. One of Dr. Leitschuh's specialties has been to work with professional service firms and their technical professionals – lawyers, accountants, engineers and consultants. Dr. Leitschuh is a licensed psychologist and holds a doctorate degree in Educational Psychology and Counseling. She speaks on an assortment of topics related to career vision, organizational leadership and enhancing human talent. She is listed in Who's Who of American Women and Who's Who of Professional Women. She is also a professional member of the National Speaker's Association.

Cheryl Leitschuh & Associates, Inc.
4468 N. Mallard Trail
Eagan, MN 55122
(651) 398-7151
E-Mail: Cheryl@career-future.com
Web: www.career-future.com

Chapter 8

Professional Development—A Lifelong Process

Micki Lewis

> "If you think of learning as a path, you can picture
> yourself walking beside her rather than either
> pushing or dragging or carrying her along."
> - Polly Berrien Berends

Personal and professional career development is an endless journey of learning. And just as learning is a path, our careers walk beside us through all the ups and downs, successes and challenges of life. Our careers are where we spend the majority of our waking moments. Keeping them in check and on the best track is a big challenge. Time, energy and money all play a part in how we keep our careers moving forward.

Let's break down all the components of the term "personal/professional career development" to get a better idea of what we're talking about:

Personal: Individual, Private, Own
Professional: Expert, Specialist, Authority
Career: Vocation, Occupation, Livelihood
Development: Progress, Advance, Improvement

Let's start with the core of this definition. The collection of all the work accomplished during one's lifetime is defined as a "career." In other words, how one chooses to spend his time in service or in a productive state can be called a career, which can span many years. Most people have several jobs under their belt over the course of a lifetime. Many have more than one career.

If we add the words "personal" and "professional" to our working definition, we think of ourselves in a business scenario, working as professionals, or experts, at what we do. The term "development" in this sense then pushes us to ask ourselves, "What methods do we use so that we may enhance or widen our career horizons?"

Taken altogether, your personal/professional career development belongs to you and is your responsibility. You alone create, implement and sustain it. Only you can strengthen and improve it to benefit your well-being. It is your personal journey, spent in service to others.

As a coach, I want to invite you to see how your career acts as your contribution to the world. Giving and receiving is part of the cycle of your life. What you give comes back to you in the form of self-satisfaction, contributions or maybe even money. How you decide to use your time and talents will determine how faithful you are to your own development.

Several studies have shown that fifty to seventy percent of workers are in the wrong job position, based on their true interests and aptitudes. This is a very scary fact that relates to the productivity of both individual workers and the companies they work for. This plays a role in how one views continuing career development.

The amount of time and energy you spend on your career development may also depend on your profession. Perhaps that dreaded continuing education that you have to keep up with looms in front of you each year. Here's a question to ask yourself: "Would I still be in the profession I am currently in if I did not have to keep the certification updated?"

For many, the value of growing and continuing to learn is encompassed by an ongoing thirst for knowledge, and the answer is a simple "yes." For others, it is a pain in the butt to have to continually take course work. "School is for the birds," they say. Or "I couldn't wait to get out of high school/college. Why should I have to continue to take training?" These comments (and others not fit for printing!) continue to surface within all organizations. These thoughts and comments are what we will address in the upcoming segments of this chapter.

If you look at your career development as a continuum, you'll see that learning is a never-ending process. Taking a look at other possible ways you might learn is a crucial step toward understanding how career development is an ongoing extension of your life.

How you view your career development through your own eyes is significant. This next segment will explore how you can continue your career development by looking through a new set of lenses. Let's just say you'll be putting on a pair of magic glasses as you look at your personal/professional career development in a new way.

The Value of Continuing Personal/Professional Career Development

The importance of career development is different to each of us. We are unique individuals, and this question can be answered differently, depending on our wants and needs. The real question we need to ask ourselves is, "What value do I place on my own continuing career development?

On a scale of one to ten, where does your commitment to the process rank? What does it mean to you? What are your priorities? Perhaps you place your family ahead of your career. Maybe you seek more balance right now. Taking a look at your past, what is the truth about your career and its continual development?

These may be extremely difficult questions to ask yourself. And there is no right way to answer each since each of us is different. At various times in your life, your priorities may have caused you to change your focus. Being flexible and open to the changes that may occur is a key to career development resilience.

When I work with clients, one of the most frequently asked questions about career development is, "What does it look like?" Most people do not have a clear picture in their minds of what it *can* look like. They seem to follow others' thoughts and dreams and rarely spend time thinking about it. Most of us spend more time researching what car to buy and planning a vacation than putting together life and career goals. (Lewis, 2003)

"I'm not young enough to know everything."
- J. M. Barrie

Some people think that learning ends with high school or college. Ahh, but that's where life really *begins*! The game of life begins to intertwine its way into our careers. Learning is then second nature; we don't even realize we are learning by living!

One thing we all have in common is the opportunity to continually learn, which doesn't always have to happen through formal education. You see, learning how to learn is a process in and of itself. And the way we learn as adults can be much more effective than the way we were taught when we were young. Adult learning takes into account our experiences and backgrounds. We get to combine all the elements and decide where we fit. It's the WIIFM (What's in it for me?) mentality! It's a purposeful education that aligns our needs with the knowledge we seek.

Your schooling may be long in the past and in need of an update. Take a look at what is really happening out there in the real world as it relates to your career development.

"The best way to predict the future is to create it."
- Peter Drucker

Planning Time

In his book *Pathfinder*, author Nicholas Lore's research indicates that sixty-eight percent of all individuals surveyed at the Rockport Institute did not know what they wanted to do with their lives and had had minimal guidance on the subject. (Lore, p. 11)

How much time have you spent developing or planning your career? This question is posed at the beginning of the career workshops I've facilitated. The majority of groups asked say they have "accidentally" fallen into their careers. They may have followed in a family member's footsteps, or friends may have invited them to work together. But it is a rare occasion that I hear someone say she has *always* wanted to be what she is!

If I ask my workshop students how well they have maintained continual career development, again, very few admit to having paid attention to the subject. I'll hear the usual responses such as, "I go to conferences" and "I attend meetings," but career development is typically not a priority to most of my students.

When the same questions are posed in small sample career surveys, the same results occur. According to the data, most of those surveyed said that if they had the chance to do it all again, they would start planning their careers in their late teens and twenties. Some experts believe that age seventeen or eighteen (and sometimes, even earlier) is the optimum time to start focusing on career development issues. While this may be the best time to create such a plan, do most people know who they are at those times of life? Have they had enough life experiences to create a path by their late teens?

There comes a time in our lives when we all ask ourselves, "What do I want to be when I grow up?" Sometimes these moments come at very pivotal times. Maybe something drastic must happen before we decide to make a change. The loss of a job or a loved one, or even not knowing ourselves very well can spur change as well. We go through many of these up and down stages in our lives. How we handle them predicts our future. Sometime during these opportunities, we ask ourselves, "Where did *I* go?" We then set out on a journey to discover who we are!

Stephen Covey, author of *The Seven Habits of Highly Effective People*, says we should be spending sixty percent of our time in the planning mode—figuring out the next steps for creating the lives or careers we desire. Input equals output, so the amount of time, energy and effort we are willing to devote to continual career development has a direct impact on the results we obtain. It's a cause-and-effect process.

The key is to put a plan together. This is one of my favorite parts of being a coach, to sit down with my clients and develop their own personal plans. To be sure, this can be an overwhelming task, with too much already on our plates and not enough time in the day. This is where we all could use some support.

Consider hiring a coach to help you with this endeavor (more on this later). It doesn't take long—just a few sessions. And a coach can also keep you on track. Have a quarterly check-in call with your coach. If you don't make a commitment to yourself to perform this task, and if you don't have any accountability, I guarantee that not much will happen. If, one year from now, you haven't planned or created your future, it will be as if you stood still, experiencing no change. All you will have done is grow a year older.

How Do You Measure Career Development?

The almighty dollar seems to have the upper hand here. Most of us justify the success of our careers with our paychecks. The majority of us think "the more, the better." But money is not always the only indicator. In fact, the monetary mindset actually seems to change as we grow older. Days off, vacation time and job satisfaction come into play later in our careers. In planning your continual career development, think about identifying these priorities in your life. Then, identify the education or skills you will need to accomplish those goals.

Along the way, you must be the final judge when it comes to career development. Celebrations and milestones are great and can give you targets and places to go. But you are the one who needs to create a vision of what you want, create the steps for how to get there, measure it consistently and continuously reflect on how you are doing.

Your Starting Point—Take Your Current Career Happiness Pulse

At this point in your career, are you happy where you are? Do you like and want to stay in your industry? Have you thought of possibly transitioning into something else? Have you had it in your heart to possibly do something else with your life/career? Are you having a hard time getting up in the morning for work? On a scale of one to ten, what is your motivation level?

How much time do you have to explore all these options? In career development, you will need to redefine, refine and reevaluate where you are on a continual basis and make the changes you feel will move you to the next level. Purchasing this book was a crucial first step in your development. Now give yourself permission to sit down, read and relish the information contained in these pages and launch your plan.

What Next?

What are your plans for continuing your journey? What do you *want* to do, and what do you *have* to do? Where you are in life now and what you want for the future will determine where you want to go. You can make plans, goals and targets to help you determine your direction.

The next section contains several techniques to guide your way. You will perform a reality check on yourself, including a career needs self-analysis, and you will also get into daily practices that will enable you to develop a strategy for success. I have included questions to ask yourself about growth opportunities and an action plan to start you on your way. Hearing about a few success stories may also enrich and show you how to create your own. Finally, we will share some quick tips for getting started on your own recycling plan.

Set your own pace. There is no right or wrong speed. Just promise to spend a generous amount of time in this preparation stage. But don't get stuck there or lose focus. This is the place to sharpen your focus. The clearer your vision, the easier it will be to take action. Write down your targets and goals and get rid of the obstacles that are in the way.

Reality Check—A Self-Assessment

Take stock of yourself. Like any smart company, you need to take inventory of yourself before you "buy" the benefits of career development. Get a professional assessment, brainstorm with others, ask for feedback—whatever method you choose, you need to know your blind spots and what you are interested in.

Career Development Timeline

One effective way to take stock of yourself is to take a look back at where you've been in your career. You can start by making a timeline (see diagrams below). This will give you an overall picture of your entire life and how it relates to ongoing and continual learning and development. Draw a line and start labeling years in groups of five to ten. You can also use a computer to create a line or use the format below. Whatever you do, leave lots of room to write and add your memories.

LIFELONG CAREER DEVELOPMENT

	Age 1-15	16-25	26-35	36-45	46-55	56-65	65+
Experiences:							
Learned:							
Life Lessons:							

Begin by identifying your years of formal education and then fill the informal education in between. Identify your informal learning according to the service, type of work or how you played a part in giving to others. Examples of early age informal training could be scouting, babysitting or helping around the house. Adult informal development could be that you were a PTA board volunteer, part of a specialized group at work, or a member of a sports team.

If you prefer you can turn the timeline on its side and begin to write across the page instead. Here's another format of how you might highlight both the formal and informal educational experiences of your life:

AGE	SPECIFIC EXPERIENCES	LEARNING	LIFE LESSONS
0-17/18	Elementary thru High School	General Studies	Discipline, Socialization
	Chores at home	Work with siblings / the value of a clean home	Trade-Offs, Responsibility, Planning, Scheduling
7-10	Swimming Lessons	Learning away from school / go on the bus	Trust in others, Risk Taking
12-15	Babysitting	Others' focus, earning money, taking "outside" class to learn	Saving Money, Goal Setting
12-14	Played on Volley Ball team	Work as a group, expectations, goal setting, disappointment, victory, motivation, competing	Teambuilding, Goals, Preparation, Celebration, Recognition, Awarded "Best Defense"
12	Scout Patrol Leader	Leadership, Negotiation, Sales, Communication, Managing	Can influence others, Interest in working with people
16-18	Leader-Physical Education	Leading in front of group	Leadership, Motivation
16-	Part time work. Full time summer work.	Working with others, office environment	Custer Service, Image, Responsibility, A REAL job!
17	Took college class in High School	College work	Real world learning, new environment
16	Lifeguard	Preparedness, Risk Taking, Prioritization, Certification	Taking Charge, Focus
18-22	College	Advanced education, More discipline, timeliness	Juggling work and school, Prioritization
22-present	Certifications	Medical and Business	Keeping up-current info, Raise my value
28	Sales Representative/Consultant	Presentations, Entrepreneurship, Salesmanship, Conflict Resolution, Self Management, Organization-al Skills, Competitiveness	Thinking out of the box, ROI, Accounting, Marketing, Building Relationships, Unique Education
30	Board Member	Dealing with difficult people	Conflict Resolution
38	College Instructor	Preparation, Instructional Design, Facilitation	Motivation, Leadership, Subject Expert
44	Author, Entrepreneur, Coach, Consultant, Speaker	Time Management, Delegation, People Skills, Needs Analysis, Communication Skills	Focus, Self-Branding, Value, Motivation, Positive Thinking, Flexibility

Recall times in your life where you truly learned through life experience, like making an important decision, moving, enduring an illness or possibly even handling a crisis. Any of these events may have shifted your focus—thus adding to your learning and development. This exercise will further demonstrate how your entire life has been a process of learning and professional development. Even if you have not gone to school formally, you have received an ongoing education nonetheless.

Is your career development timeline a straight one? Probably not. It more likely resembles a series of ocean waves. You'll notice times where immense learning took place and other times where things seemed to stagnate. When you look at the big picture of your personal and professional development, view it as a broad process of learning, and then the storms of change may seem a little less threatening.

You can also use the timeline to project your career's future. Start with your retirement and work backward. What do you want, what do you want to learn, how long will it take and what are the steps in getting there? Remember, as the retirement age continues to increase, your timeline will always be changing.

If you take a hard look at your life you'll see how you have always been learning and educating yourself. The time it took to learn and hone all these skills was not short—it has been an ongoing process throughout your life.

When working with clients, I find that **time** is always a major concern. I am frequently asked, "How much time is my career development going to take? How can I fit it into my schedule? Will there be time for me to do this later in life?"

The challenge is that we give so much to others that we rarely have time for ourselves. When was the last time you just sat and did nothing or did something selfish, just for yourself? Most of us battle the incessant busyness of life such as errands, house cleaning, yard work and social committees. But remember: We are human beings—not human doings!

Let me put the time drain dilemma into perspective. When flight attendants on airplanes demonstrate how the oxygen masks work, they instruct adult passengers to put their own masks on first and then that of the children. This illustration shows that sometimes your actual survival depends on taking care of yourself first...then others!

The same applies to our personal and professional lives. You probably know someone who gives so much to others that they can barely take care of themselves. Are you one of those people? Now is the time to give yourself time for *you*.

> "Most people will look back and realize they did not
> have a great life because it's so easy to
> settle for a good life."
> - Jim Collins

STRATEGIES FOR SUCCESS

Identify Personal and Professional Goals

What are your goals and intentions for the next year? At the end of every year or early each new year, our family sits down together, and we discuss what we want for the upcoming year. We make three lists—one for our home, one for our relationships and one for ourselves. I have found that when we don't take the time to write down our goals, nothing happens the next year!

Note, however, that there is a difference between an intention and a goal. In the dictionary, the word "intention" is defined as, "A settled direction of the mind toward the doing of a certain act." If we create our intentions first, then the goals will emerge. A goal is defined as, "A point or points toward which effort or movement is directed; an aim, a focus." Goals are set as milestones along the paths of our intentions.

Here is a personal example of my intentions for this year:
- to be the best model for self and others
- to acknowledge, utilize and bestow my inherent talents
- to be bold and step outside into a new world

All my decisions are based around these intentions. My goals, therefore, stem from my intentions. One goal might be:
- to be healthy, generous and have a strong commitment to myself on a daily basis.

Breaking this goal down into more detail would include exercising, eating healthily and taking five minutes a day for personal think time. (In coaching we call it "executive think time." We are the executives of our own lives, so let's create the space.)

Check Your Attitude

What is more important—skills or attitudes? First, we should distinguish the difference between the two. One *learns* skills; on the other hand, one *has* a great attitude.

Zig Ziglar shares a wonderful exercise for understanding what is more important—skills or attitudes. As a career coach, I encourage clients to put themselves in the shoes of others, asking, "If you were a hiring manager, what would you look for in an employee?" The majority of the answers given usually reflect desired sets of attitudes. Now ask yourself, "Would I like to have someone working for me who has skills but is angry and negative?" I suspect your answer would be "Absolutely not!"

"Opportunity is missed by most people because it
is dressed in overalls and it looks like work.
- Thomas Edison

Self-Upgrade

Ask yourself, "What skills do I need to move forward in my life? Do I really have to go back to school in order to learn these new skills?" The answers may be surprising. Upgrading skills is just a part of the overall strategy for supporting your continual career development.

Taking off the Blinders: Trend Watching

It blows me away when people don't know what is happening in the world outside their work. How many of us pick up *American Demographics* magazine or any of the trend-watch books that are out there? Few, no doubt. The majority of us live in our own little worlds.

One of the best things you can do for your career is be a trend watcher. Information can be easily found by looking at the latest magazines as well as what is going on outside your personal field and how it relates to your industry. Use your local newspaper or city magazine to learn what 's really happening in your area. It can be such a great asset to your company, your team and yourself.

Getting Help

But you can't make your journey alone. Who can support your quest for a career development strategy? Who have you used in the past to help you get where you want? How have you found meaningful work in the past? Where have you gone for fun and enjoyment?

While friends and family may be the first people you turn to for help, I recommend that you seek assistance from a career professional. Friends are wonderful to have, but is your best friend a professional whom you will trust to advise you on the most important aspects of your life, career and/or business? A professional can help you much faster than family or friends. And being open to outside help is smart because your family and friends have too much bias and too much at stake to jeopardize your relationship. They may not always tell you what you need to hear. My advice: Have a best friend *and* seek professional career help.

Career professionals include consultants, therapists, mentors and coaches. Which can help you the most? What are the differences between them?

Consultant. A consultant is called in as an expert to find solutions to a particular problem. Coaching can be seen as a form of consulting, yet the coach stays with the client to implement new skills, changes and goals to ensure results.

Therapist. Coaches are not therapists. Coaches don't work on "issues" or get into the past or deal much with understanding human behavior. Those things are best left up to the client to figure out with a therapist. Coaches can help clients move forward and set personal and professional goals that will give you a more enjoyable life.

Mentor. A mentor is usually a support individual inside a corporation who assists inexperienced workers with understanding corporate politics, career advancement and learning crucial information for moving forward within that particular organization.

Coach. A coach gets you where you want to be more quickly than you could by yourself. You can use a coach for your career, your business or your life. A coach can also refer you to a specialist.

"There is very little traffic on the "extra" mile.
- Anonymous

Keep Reaching

How far are we reaching to stay in development mode? There are times in our lives when it may not be as far as we might need. Life gets in the way! Continue to reevaluate how you spend your time in continual career development. There is no limit to your potential for reaching the next step.

A famous song by Gladys Knight and the Pips says, "We have to use our imagination to keep on keeping on." This should be your mantra for continual career development. Keep plugging away, always, and use your imagination to help you continue.

How much risk taking are you willing to venture? Depending on your situation, it could be a lot or virtually none. Those who do take more risks seem to get further ahead in life. Do you have a fearless focus—that is, a specific focus that knows no fear? You must be fearless.

Don't attach yourself to the outcome, so that whether you are successful or not, it's no big deal!

Be Prepared

Whatever you do, wherever you go, you will always hear this saying: "The key is to be prepared." In fact, our entire lives have probably either worked or not worked based on our levels of preparedness. Studies have found that those who prepare are less likely to have chronic career problems. Those with monetary reserves are ready when a major financial obstacle emerges. Having knowledge and doing nothing with it is a waste! You must take action to be prepared for whatever come your way. Yes, it takes work to be prepared.

Ask yourself these questions:
1. What skills do I need to get where I want?
2. What research do I need to conduct to get there?
3. What is my timeline for accomplishing my goals?

These questions will put you in the frame of mind needed to gather skills for growth. Are you willing to go the extra mile?

"No one ever achieved greatness
by playing it safe."
- Harry Gray

Being Too Comfortable

One client in particular was "shocked" and could not believe they could let her go when she was laid off. She believed she was in a "safe" place and the company had finished with the restructuring. She thought she wouldn't be " touched."

Needless to say many of us can be in this same predicament right at this moment. My advice is to get prepared for the worst case scenario. Financial Planners state it would be wise to have six months worth of cash reserve—JUST IN CASE!

Often, we become too comfortable when times are predictable. When you are comfortable, however, is when you need to be on the lookout. It is extremely smart to get your antennae up and see what is going on around you. It's at these times you need to have a higher amount of awareness.

Proactive Vs. Reactive

What is your strategy? Are you in a reactive state—a participant in your own personal professional career development? Or are you being proactive, preparing ahead of time for the "What ifs?" We all know how being reactive can be detrimental to our careers. The experience is not pleasant. It's very uncomfortable.

So what are you doing to be proactive? How do you start to become more proactive with your career development? Where do you want to be, and how are you going to accomplish it? Start today! Get the calendar, start finding places to learn and create the career of your dreams.

Break Time/Think Time

Allowing yourself to have some "think time" or taking a much-needed break away from your career is good. Call it a sabbatical and everyone you know will be envious! The amount of time you actually sit and plan is very important. Just be sure to have a timeline for when you will re-ignite your personal/career development and plan accordingly.

Movement

Check the pace at which your career development is moving. Do you want it to flow easily like a smooth river or behave like white rapids—dangerous and scary? It is your choice, and it depends on how fast you want to move forward in your career. Identifying the importance of moving faster or slower will enable you to plan much more wisely.

Seeing career development as an endless flow or being limitless is valuable. It helps you know that it is always there. Just as lifelong learning begins as soon as we are born, our career development stays alongside us throughout our entire lives.

Walt Disney said, "Somehow, I can't believe there are many heights that can't be scaled by a man who knows the secret of making dreams come true." This special outlook can be "summarized with four Cs: curiosity, confidence, courage and constancy. The greatest of these is confidence."

"A great pleasure in life is doing what
people say you cannot do."
- Walter Gagehot

Incorporate Possibility

Have you learned about incorporating possibility into the next step of your continual career development? Have you dared to dream and think of what could be? It is extremely important to keep dreams alive. Walt Disney and Albert Einstein are prime examples of this in the way they lived their lives. John F. Kennedy unleashed the possibility of going to the moon with only a speech.

So what might you dream about? Don't look at it as an overwhelming task; use a coach to help you co-create your plan and start the momentum needed to succeed.

Career Development—More Than Just Conferences

If you think continuing career development consists of nothing more than attending conferences, you are dead wrong. Sure, that's one way of keeping in tune with your industry, but take a second or third look around. What can you do on a daily basis to improve and continue your career development? What can you pull out of your back pocket? Where else can you upgrade your career?

Are You Making Continual Contacts?

You may not have kept up with your colleagues or maintained your relationships with them, but check in with them at least once a year, even if it's just to catch up. How well do you keep up with your contacts? It's amazing how often we'll call on them only when we need them instead of just calling to say "Hello."

If it has been a while since you contacted your buddies or colleagues, do so right now. Make one or two phone calls per week to stay in touch with those who may (or even those who may not) be of support right now. You never know when you may need someone. If you haven't kept up with your card file, you may want to do that now, or use the computer to set up a system. You never know what may happen, and you always want to be prepared.

"The more I learn, the more I realize I don't know" -
- Albert Einstein

Be On The Lookout

Paying attention to yourself is a major key to a successful career. The higher your awareness, the more keenly you will be able to look at yourself. Be consistent and open to any way you can update your self-awareness. As a coach, I continually ask my clients, "What don't you know? What would be good to investigate so you can be ahead of others in your field?" Albert Einstein's quote above hits home here. Keep your nose sniffing to seek out what is happening. Ask yourself what you're yearning to learn. What keeps whispering in your ear or nudging you in your side?

> "Try not to become a man of success, but rather to become a man of value. He is considered successful in our day who gets more out of life than he puts in. But a man of value will give more than he receives."
> – Albert Einstein

How can you be of value? Think outside the box when it comes to continuing your career development. Try volunteering or mentoring young people. If you have skills to teach a subject, do so, and the rewards will be unbelievable. It's amazing how much we can be of value to others and share our strengths.

For additional reading and resources, please refer to these publications.

Stephen Covey, *The Seven Habits of Highly Effective People*

Nicholas Lore, *Pathfinder*

William Bridges, *Transitions*

Zig Ziglar, Various books and tapes

Micki Lewis, *How Clear is Your Vision*

Ben and Roz Zander, *The Art of Possibility*

Micki Lewis

National Speaker and Coach Micki Lewis has inspired organizations and individuals for over two decades. Her unique flair for co-creating enthusiasm with over 10,000 workshop participants in technical, medical and business/career arenas has provided performance improvement and high ROI both internally and externally. Additionally, Micki has coached over 600 clients shifting each to higher levels in career and/or business success. Blending a degree in Organizational Leadership as well as being certified as a Professional Coach (PCC) from the International Coach Federation (ICF), Lewis uses cutting edge tools to engage those who to choose to upgrade their talents and boost their environment. Micki has accumulated numerous awards of excellence and high achievements in sales, teamwork and communication. Ms. Lewis continues to retain her ophthalmic certifications (ABOC, COA) as well as being a Certified Professional Values and Behavioral Analyst (CPVA, CPBA). A graduate of Coach University and licensed coaching facilitator with Corporate Coach University, Lewis is also a member of CC-ASTD, the American Society for Training and Development and is a Registered Organizational Development Professional (RODP).

3 FACETS Micki Lewis is known for:
Gets clients to FAST FOCUS
LIGHTS A FIRE under them if need be!
IS lots of FUN!!!

Micki Lewis
ENVISION RESULTS, Inc.
Box 550, Naperville, IL 60566
(630) 561-2071, Office
(630) 305-9115, Fax
Coaching Hotline: (630) 357-5730
E-mail: mlewis@envisionresults.com
www.envisionresults.com

Chapter 9

Solid Communication—The Foundation for Successful Job Interviews

Steven Friedman

Most companies find that employee turnover and career development are among their biggest challenges. And as employees look to either change workplaces altogether or move to other positions within their current organizations, the interview process poses particular challenges—not just for the job candidates themselves but for the managers who are looking to fill the vacant positions.

Good communication by both parties is a must in any job interview situation. To better understand the challenges that result from poor communication, it is necessary to comprehend exactly how things can go wrong. It is also important to see how career development strategies can develop once good communication systems are in place.

The purpose of this chapter is to give you a sense of how easily things can go wrong when bad communication exists in interviews. We will also discuss strategies for correcting mistakes—both on the part of the candidate and of the person doing the interview—so that mutual success is possible.

To get a sense of the impact that bad communication can have on an interview, consider the following scenario.

The Average Interview

Heather is going on an interview because she has decided that she must change her job. It is a serious pursuit for her, and her dream is to get hired. To say the least, she is feeling pressure and is nervous. She desires a good job fit, with plenty of opportunities to advance her career, develop her abilities and help her grow personally and professionally. Since this job is important to her, she knows that first impressions are crucial, so she dresses in a great interview suit. She wants to like the person with whom she is interviewing, and she hopes to sell him on her potential value to the company so that ultimately, she will get a job offer.

The gentleman doing the hiring, Mark, also has many things on his agenda. There is an overdue meeting to discuss budget cuts, complaints from three customers that need attention and negotiations on a major contract that must be resolved because of the revenue that account creates for the company. And of course, there is the interview to fill that job opening in his department.

For Mark, putting the right person in the position is important; doing so will ultimately make his life easier by helping him get more done in a more timely fashion. Plus, he knows he must improve his bottom line by six percent this quarter, and the new hire is vital to achieving that result. The day has so many pressure points already, Mark tells himself, that perhaps the interview can be put aside. But on the other hand, the position needs to be filled tomorrow, so maybe she can agree on the spot to join the company and start soon. There are so many issues involved in his decision, that he feels anxiety about finding the solution.

Heather is feeling anxious as well. And she has reason to be nervous. Other than a browse through the company web site and some brief conversation about the position as she set up the appointment, she has had very little assistance from Mark in preparing for the interview. She is focused on presenting herself well but is going in almost cold.

When she arrives for the interview, she is told to go to the eighth floor reception area and ask for Mark. Further instructions will be waiting for her there. When she arrives, the regular receptionist gets up and leaves for her break while another person covers for her. Heather presents herself to this new person, who has no idea what to do since there is no written message to relay. She suggests that Heather wait until the regular receptionist comes back. When Heather mentions that she is there to meet with Mark, she is told that his line is busy. So she is forced to wait. A few minutes later, when she tries again, she is told that the line is still busy. So she sits and waits again.

After twenty minutes, the regular receptionist arrives back at the desk. Only then does Heather learn that Mark was to have been voice paged and that he would have come right out had he known she was there. Finally, Mark is paged and appears a few minutes later, dressed in a company logo oxford shirt and khaki pants that are befitting the company's casual dress code.

"Hi, I'm Mark Stevens. I had expected you about twenty minutes ago. Is everything okay? You know, professionalism and timeliness are important values here, so I hope this is not the way you go about your business. Come on. Let's go back to my office, but I have to apologize in advance. I had assumed we would have about thirty-five minutes or more together, and now that you are twenty minutes late, we may be a bit rushed. I have another appointment scheduled in just a few minutes."

As he takes a seat behind his desk and points to an open chair for Heather, Mark describes what he hopes to accomplish by filling the vacant position.

"This is an important position. We have had flat revenues over a period of time, and this quarter alone, I must increase results by at least six percent. I read over your resume, and it certainly reveals some of the attributes we are looking for. So, Heather, tell me about yourself."

"I have been in my current position for three years," she begins. "I have just completed the second year of my MBA program, alternating weekends—"

She is interrupted by the phone. Mark answers, cutting her off in mid syllable.

The conversation, which goes on for about five minutes, is one that Heather knows she should not be overhearing since it involves the way another associate is handling her responsibilities. Heather sits patiently.

When Mark finally hangs up, he says, "I know you were in the middle of telling me about your current job, but let me tell you what is going on here. First, there is tremendous pressure on us. Our division had been a superstar on the project team, always generating results that were eleven to fifteen percent higher than our peer teams. And our revenue rate was tops. The challenge is that our new senior vice president has it in for our team, I guess. He is trying hard to raise our standards of performance, but in reality, he just does not understand at all how our customers see us. We need to achieve a huge, six-percent increase before the end of the quarter, and he is not giving us the support to achieve it. He has consolidated two positions, redefined another and is asking for certain benchmarks without regard to what we have done in the past."

Mark's rant goes on for a few more minutes before he returns to his original line of conversation. "Tell me about what you have been doing," he probes again. As Heather starts to answer, the phone rings again—this time, a five-minute call in which she overhears details of project challenges, the reasons why it is over budget and an earnest admonishment to the person on the other end of the phone. After hanging up, Mark says, "Based upon your resume, you really are perfect. In fact, I knew this interview would be just a formality, and it certainly has confirmed my hopes. We have a job open that is yours if you would like it. You can start Monday."

Heather is a bit stunned, since she has said so little. She has hardly had a chance to ask questions or give Mark the chance to learn anything about her. She feels as if she has hardly had an interview at all, yet she has been offered the position. Mark hurriedly stands, offers his hand and says, "Heather, I will call personnel, and they will work out the details with you. I am running late, so let's pick a starting date that is as soon as possible!"

This is hardly a successful presentation and, unfortunately, not an unusual occurrence in the workplace. It depicts a person who does not know how to interview, how to select a candidate or make the interviewee feel comfortable.

Let's look at all of the mistakes that took place in this previous scenario. Notice how Heather was poorly prepared for the interview. She received little advance notice about what to expect and as a result was justifiably in the dark about a great many things. She came into present herself in a professional manner and did not even get the chance. Also notice that Mark wasn't nearly as focused on Heather as he should have been, given his position. His behavior was typical of a stressed out manager.

Now, lets' start over and present another way that Mark and Heather could have handled this job interview:

The Improved Interview

Mark has his eye on two candidates, whose resumes have been sent to him based upon the recommendations of friends. He has settled on these two because of their solid backgrounds. They both seem to have the potential for success within his division. Knowing that career development issues begin with a mutually successful interview process, Mark wants to ensure that the interviews are conducted professionally.

He calls one of the candidates, Heather, to schedule an interview. "Hello, Heather, this is Mark Stevens. I have your resume in front of me, and based upon a brief review of your achievements, I believe that you might be a valid candidate for the opening we have in our division.

"Before we get together, however, it is important for me to tell you how this process will work so you can feel as comfortable as possible. The interview will consist of at least two meetings. Our first meeting will truly be a 'compatibility meeting' to help you understand a few things about our organization—how we operate, what the position will involve and how you might become a part of it.

"It is also important for me to get to know you personally—in addition to your career vision and scope of performance—so we both can feel comfortable that a process is in place that will support the goals of the team. Heather, am I making sense so far?

Heather answers affirmatively, and Mark continues: "At our second meeting, I will review in detail the profit expectations that come with your position, the strategies that you will be implementing and the courses of action that will be critical to your success if we both decide that our team is the right place for you. How does this all sound to you?"

Heather is relieved to know that Mark is being serious and careful about the interview process. It seems to make good sense.

"Heather," Mark continues, "if this makes sense, then I would like you to do two things. First, tour our company web site and find out as much about our projects, and us, as possible. When you come in, feel prepared to explain how your background matches up with what you learned about us. In addition, I would like you to read through some material that I will send you before the interview. How does that sound?"

Heather realizes that performance is required in order to get this position. She knows she is qualified but still feels a twinge of panic as she realizes that she will need to perform well in the interview to get hired. She feels she is being tested.

Two days before the interview, as he has promised, Mark e-mails Heather some information about the company, its current projects and other pertinent information. She hopes she will learn enough from this information, as well as the company web site, to know if her background matches up with the requirements of the position.

When Heather arrives on the day of the interview, the person at the reception desk tells her that Mark will be out in a moment to greet her. He arrives promptly and leads her not to his office but to a conference room. He also brings along a laptop computer to facilitate the meeting.

"Heather, I must pay you a compliment. Based upon our discussion so far, you clearly present yourself as a detailed and disciplined individual."

Heather responds with a simple "Thank you."

"Of the information you have reviewed from our web site and from what was e-mailed to you, what has gotten you the most excited about our organization?" Mark queries.

"It is clear that the company has direction and focus, and I was excited about how technology has partnered with your customer base to keep you abreast of their wants and needs. I was also impressed with the perception your customers have of your products based on internal surveys."

Mark then confirms what Heather has just said. "So if I hear you correctly, you feel that our technology base and the directions we have focused on seem consistent with the perceptions of our client base. And that is important to you. Am I on target?"

"Yes."

"Heather, what are your expectations of our meeting today, and what would you like the outcome to be?"

"Mr. Stevens, I see this meeting as a chance for us to get to know each other and for me to learn about the projects that I could potentially be hired to participate in. In addition, it gives us both a chance to see how my background will help you here so I might ultimately get an offer from you."

"So you want us to get to know each other, and you would like to learn about the projects we are involved in and see how they match your skills. Then, if those skills do match, you would like us to move toward the affiliation phase. Am I on target here?'

Heather agreed that he was.

Positive Steps

Let's recap the three simple steps that Mark has taken thus far:
1. He greeted Heather, paid her a compliment and led her to an appropriate meeting space.
2. He broke the ice.
3. He asked her the Big Question and clarified their mutual goals.

First, Mark paid Heather a business compliment, pointing out something about her that initially would make her feel great about the business relationship they might build. He paid attention to her business background and complimented her about that. This is vital because it helped establish confidence and rapport with Heather.

The next step Mark took was discovering quickly what Heather had learned about the company. He had sent her material and asked her to come to the interview prepared. He also wanted to make sure she had done her homework. These actions, in turn, gave Heather the sense that Mark was interested in her thoughts on and opinions of the organization.

Finally, Mark asked Heather what she wanted to accomplish at the meeting. This is the so-called Big Question: "What are your expectations?" Heather's answer helped Mark understand what her goals really were and gave both of them the chance to clarify their respective expectations of the meeting. In addition, the question and answer gave both Mark and Heather a road map for how to develop a strategy for their time together. This built confidence on both sides of the interview table.

Note also that the meeting took place in a conference room—not in the interviewer's office, across a desk. This was important because any interview should take place in neutral territory, and conference rooms usually meet that criterion.

Now let's go back to the interview…

Mark explains to Heather how the interview process will operate. He delivers a Power Point presentation on how he will work with her throughout the interview, how different his company is from other organizations that she might interview with and how the interview will be a two-phase process. He tells her that the first phase will focus on their respective accountabilities and that the second phase will deal with their business relationship, what that relationship might mean to company projects and the overall profitability of the organization.

With the interview now underway, Marks works a number of behavioral questions into the process. These kinds of questions fall into a variety of categories, with no right or wrong answers. Behavioral questions take hypothetical situations and put people into the scenarios to see how each job candidate would respond and deal with that situation. People bring certain values to the way they think through situations. These thoughts become evident, and it helps establish benchmarks for mutual success and communication. That then helps build success in developing a long-range fit.

Some of the behavioral question categories one might use are:
- Service, working within guidelines
- Integrity, honesty, trustworthiness
- Personality, temperament, ability to work with others
- Learning from past mistakes
- Creativity, creative thinking, problem solving

In any interview scenario there has to be an emphasis on who is in charge. The person in charge dominates the questions and is assertive in the conversation. In fact, it is not unusual in an interview for the one doing all of the answering to be the one who is more exhausted when the meeting is over.

But while traditional wisdom holds that the interviewer does most of the asking, it is not unusual for an interviewee to take charge as effectively as the interviewer. In fact, I recommend it. Candidates look impressive when they lead the conversation and take charge. Although it may seem odd for the interviewee to take control, it is the best way to truly demonstrate interest and knowledge. This also strengthens the interviewer's opinion of the candidate as there is a sense that she is extremely interested in learning about the organization. This is a win-win approach.

Imagine if Heather had asked Mark these two questions: "Mr. Stevens, of the materials that you e-mailed me and the web site information, what could I have focused on specifically that would have been of value to you?" or "Mr. Stevens, what would you like to accomplish in our meeting today so that it is of value to you?"

Notice that Mark actually asked Heather these very same questions earlier, but by asking them herself, Heather has set the pace for the dialogue. This is what most interviewers never see, and it can, in fact, set the candidate apart from the competition.

Effective Questions

Let's examine the many behavioral questions that Mark—and even Heather, in some cases—can ask. Then we'll consider some of the answers that might be given. As noted earlier, there are several categories of questions, which focus on different situations that may occur. Again, the point of these questions is to determine how a person thinks through a variety of situations. There are no correct answers, yet the way the person answers is clearly related to her values and business thinking.

Questions about service and working within guidelines:

- In the past, how have you given outstanding service when involved with a client or customer?
- Is there anything about the way you work now that bothers you the most?
- If you could wave a magic wand, how would you change your present environment?
- What personal qualities do you think would make you successful here? How do you demonstrate those?
- Has there been a time when you pulled your team together in the midst of a difficult situation?
- Tell me about a time when your team fell apart. Why did it happen? What did you do?

Questions to reveal integrity, honesty, trustworthiness:

- Discuss a time when your integrity was challenged. How did you handle it?
- What would you do if someone asked you to do something unethical?
- Have you ever asked for forgiveness for doing something wrong?
- In what business situations do you feel honesty would be appropriate?
- If you saw a co-worker doing something dishonest, would you tell your boss? What would you do about it?

Questions to reveal personality, temperament, the ability to work with others:

- What brings you joy?
- If you took out a full-page ad in the *New York Times* and had to describe yourself in only three words, what would they be?
- How would you describe your personality?
- What motivates you the most?
- If I call your references, what will they say about you?
- Do you consider yourself a risk taker? Describe a situation in which you had to take a risk.
- What kind of environment would you like to work in?
- What kinds of responsibilities would you like to have in your next job?

- What are two or three examples of tasks that you do not particularly enjoy doing? Indicate how you remain motivated to complete those tasks.
- What kinds of people bug you?
- Tell me abut a work situation that irritated you.
- Have you ever had to resolve a conflict with a co-worker or client? How did you resolve it?
- Describe the appropriate relationship between a supervisor and subordinates.
- What sort of relationships do you have with your associates, both at your level and those above and below you?
- How have you worked as a member of teams in the past?
- Tell me about some of the groups you've had to get cooperation from. What did you do?
- What is you management style? How do you think your subordinates receive you?
- As a manager, have you ever had to fire anyone? If so, what were the circumstances, and how did you handle it?
- Have you ever been in a situation where a project was returned for errors? What effect did this have on you?
- What previous job was the most satisfying? Why?
- What job was the most frustrating? Why?
- Tell me about the best boss you ever had. Now tell me about your worst boss. What made it tough to work for him or her?
- What do you think you owe to your employer?
- What does you employer owe to you?

Questions to reveal past mistakes:

- Tell me about an objective in your last job that you failed to meet? Why did you fail?
- When is the last time you were criticized? How did you deal with it?
- What have you learned from your mistakes?
- Tell me about a situation in which you abruptly had to change what you were doing.
- If you could change one managerial decision you made during the past two years, what would that be?
- Tell me of a time when you had to work on a project that didn't work out the way it should have. What did you do?

- If you had the opportunity to change anything in your career, what would you have done differently?

Questions to reveal creativity, creative thinking and problem solving:

- When was the last time you "broke the rules" by thinking outside the box? How did you do it?
- What have you done that was innovative?
- What was the wildest idea you had in the past year? What did you do about it?
- Give me an example of when someone brought you a new idea, particularly one that was odd or unusual. What did you do?
- If you could do anything in the world, what would you do?
- Describe a situation in which you had a difficult management problem. How did you solve it?
- What is the most difficult decision you've had to make? How did you arrive at your decision?
- Describe some situations in which you worked under pressure or met deadlines.
- Were you ever in a situation in which you had to meet two different deadlines given to you by two different people and you couldn't do both? What did you do?
- What type of approach to solving work problems seems to work best for you? Give me an example of when you solved a tough problem.
- When taking on a new task, do you like to have a great deal of feedback and responsibility at the outset, or do you like to try your own approach?
- You're on the phone with another department resolving a problem. The intercom pages you with a customer on hold. Your manager returns your monthly report with red pen markings and demands corrections within the hour. Which do you do?
- Describe a sales presentation when you had the right product/service, and the customer wanted it but wouldn't buy it. What did you do next?
- What kind of management style do you prefer?
- Why are you seeking a new position?
- What are you looking for in an office?
- What kind of training is the most important to you?

- What kind of environment are you looking for?
- Is there anyone else giving you input on this decision?
- What seem to be the positive aspects of this organization so far?
- What will define success for you?
- How much time will you commit to achieving that goal?
- How soon will you make a decision?

In addition to the categories of behavioral questions we've covered so far, **here are a few miscellaneous questions** that would enhance the effectiveness of a job interview dialogue:

- How do you measure your own success?
- What is the most interesting thing you've done in the past three years?
- What are your short-term and long-term career goals?
- Why should we hire you?
- What responsibilities do you want, and what kinds of results do you expect to achieve in your next job?
- What do you think it takes to be successful in a company like ours?
- How did the best manager you ever had motivate you to perform well? Why did the method work?
- What is the best thing a previous employer did that you wish everyone did?
- What are you most proud of?
- What is important to you in a job?
- What do you expect to find in our company that you don't have now?
- Is there anything you wanted me to know about you that we haven't discussed?
- Do you have any questions for me?

Although this is a hearty list, there are still more questions that truly create a lot of potential for discussion. Imagine if Mark asks Heather, "When was the last time you broke the rules?" This is a great question because it creates a discussion of what the rules are in the first place, who set them and what about them requires that they be broken. It is a wonderful place to enter into discussion about how projects might get tackled and what that impending result could mean. It also gives a sense of how problems can get solved. Other great questions to ask are, "When do you think dishonesty is inappropriate?" and "What do you owe your supervisor?"

Again, questions do not necessarily have to be posed by the interviewer alone; they can be asked by the candidate as well. Imagine Heather asking a few: "What is it like when projects are returned for errors around here? How do people react?" "Was the staff ever in a situation in which it had to meet two different deadlines given by two different people and they couldn't do both? What did they do?" "What do you feel you owe those who report to you?"

Finally, after asking his own questions, Mark must summarize what he has heard: "Heather, we have had a great deal of conversation today. What I would like to do is summarize what I have learned about you as it relates to this situation. First you are most excited about ___. As I have heard, your biggest concern in this potential transition is ___.

And you feel best, potentially, about ___. Am I on target?"

The best part about this exchange is that it enables the candidate to summarize her comments for the supervisor.

In summary; if the interview process is set up to measure compatibility and assess how two people can come together to create revenue and profit, a win-win scenario can happen for both parties. Preparation is the key! Reviewing and remembering the scenarios above can help you achieve that realm of success.

Steven Friedman

In 1989 my boss said to me, "Steve we just do not like the color of your neck tie; so whenever you want, leave!" From that piece of guidance came an opportunity to reinvent myself. Consulting became a new way of life out of the corporate ashes. Using sales management experiences in a Fortune 500 company had value in industries that had less structure than the one I had been in. Using skills of how to hire effectively, getting those hired to produce at exceptional levels; and creating a vision where clients could retain more people because of the hiring systems created others to frequently involve this winning process and learn from one that had understood first hand. For over ten years Steve has been associated with the most successful recruiting programs nationally; has been accepted as a staff member of the REAL TRENDS ACADEMY; is a member of the National Speakers Association; and his retreats have earned him a 94% satisfaction rate among attendees nationally. Steve is widely published national resource to top sales organizations. In short, Steve dynamically creates a system that works to build profit through career development and hiring. This process and coaching system has changed the way organizations have gone about the recruiting and career development scenario; both in the profit and non-profit sector. He is a member of several non-profit boards. Steve's clients include Coldwell Banker; Long and Foster; John L. Scott; RE/MAX; Prudential and many major affiliates in major market places around the United States. He has two books about to be published this fall; *I'm Cold, You Need A Sweater*, and *100 Business Adages Learned from my Jewish Mother*.

Steven Friedman
Recruiting Services Inc.
P.O. Box 2667
Kensington, MD 20891
1-800-253-2044
www.stevefriedman.com

Chapter 10

Don't Let Good Principles of Success Stand in the Way of Great Ones

Marilyn Schott

Have you tried to get into your peak mind set?

Have you tried to find your personal power?

Have you tried living your life with passion?

Some people say, "The word 'try' is an excuse, used by some to attempt to justify their lack of accomplishments."

Do you want cutting-edge, results-producing principles to jump-start your career and personal life? You can have them easily and effortlessly, whether you're in sales, in management or in the financial or legal arena. Even if you are an entrepreneur, I guarantee you will become an even better one if you follow these simple, powerful and useful principles to elevate your life to the next level. We all want to believe in shortcuts, unlimited power and magic so much that sometimes we ignore the obvious things that stare us right in the face.

I'm sure you have purchased other career development books before buying this one. Apparently, the other books didn't work. So why will this chapter be different and cause real change or success for you? Because you will take a new approach. Because you want something different and better in your career and life. This chapter can be the fulcrum for making those changes, but only if you do some things differently. I recommend that you don't read this material passively. Instead, to help create that incredible life for yourself, keep a journal close at hand to take notes and write out what your burning desire is.

"If one advances confidently in the direction of his own dreams, and endeavors to live the life which he has imagined, he will meet with a success unexpected in common hours."
- Henry David Thoreau

One of my clients wanted real success. Cathy had what I call a burning desire for prosperity, happiness and health. Every day, she used the tested principles that I'm about to share with you. She went from being the number ten sales person to number three in less than four months. Throughout all of 2002, this woman remained at either the number three or number four level in her sales unit. Needless to say, she won several awards because of her productivity, even selling products with which she had previously not had much success.

We talked about the reason for her success. I asked her, "Now that you have financial success, how does it make you feel?" She said she felt peaceful, light-hearted and had fewer worries. She said because of her focus at work, she and her husband were getting along better. She added that her health was excellent, that she had less stress and even found time to exercise, which gave her a great sense of confidence and boosted her energy level.

Do you want similar things in your life? Have they been eluding you? Are you prepared to put all your heart and mind into an alert awareness? Are you ready to experience some feelings and emotions? You might be asking, "Why do I have to experience feelings and emotions?" It is because emotions are behind the actions that can either lead us to further despair or toward what we really want out of life. Someone experiencing despair might say, "I guess I don't have a choice in this situation" or "I have to work overtime to pay the bills." Someone who sees her emotions in a positive light might say, "When I took this job, I knew the hours would allow me to pursue my deepest desire, that of spending quality time with my children." Look at the emotions and feelings behind each of these experiences. Are your feelings trapping you or setting you free?

Here are the principles that I, as well as many of my clients, have found to be the secrets to a successful life and career:

PRINCIPLE ONE
Having a burning desire creates focus.

PRINCIPLE TWO
Energy fuels focus.

PRINCIPLE THREE
Positive self-talk creates a positive reality.

PRINCIPLE FOUR
Visualization shapes reality.

PRINCIPLE FIVE
Decluttering the space around you allows
more energy to come to you.

PRINCIPLE SIX
The written word can lead to a manifest reality.

PRINCIPLE SEVEN
Exercise and nutrition create self-confidence,
energy and productivity.

Until a life-threatening illness hit me, I had never practiced these principles faithfully every day. As a result, my life was great one year and not so great the next. I found, however, that the principles must be practiced every day to get results. A deliberate pattern must be established if they are to work.

I really wish someone had grabbed my attention with the answers when I was in my twenties. Perhaps they did and I failed to see the importance of consistency. That's why I am excited that you are ready to receive these principles of success.

Let's take a closer look at the principles and see how they may be different than those you are currently following.

PRINCIPLE ONE
Having a burning desire creates focus.

Do you have a burning desire to do something, something so compelling you think about it all day and all night? You've got to have a burning desire! It's difficult for someone to give this feeling to you. It's similar to passion. You must have passion in order to give it to others; similarly, you must have a burning desire in order to attract what you really want from life.

A desire is defined in the dictionary as a craving, a longing— something you yearn, hunger or thirst for. Imagine, then, how we might describe a *burning* desire. That's even more potent than a simple desire. It is a huge feeling of want! Have you experienced this?

Note that a burning desire is not like desperation, which implies acting in a reckless, wild or frantic manner. Desperation describes a negative connotation of desire. Notice how you feel when you just say the word "desperate." Doesn't feel so good, does it?

Think about that new red car, a new house, an increase in pay, being number one on the team, that fulfilling job, that new coat. The list could go on and on. Use your journal now to write down the things that you really, really want, and then find the underlying reasons for wanting these things. Do they make you feel safe, peaceful, joyful or justified?

You can create a burning desire every day. It's your choice. It's important that you are doing what you love. If you don't love what you're doing, it is more difficult to create a true burning desire.

You can even fake a burning desire until you really get it because your subconscious mind does not understand whether the emotions and thoughts you're dealing with are real or not. If you tell yourself that you have a burning desire for something often enough, your subconscious mind will eventually believe it. What I'm talking about here are not just affirmations. Your desire must represent a clear picture of what you want. It should be accompanied by the same feelings and emotions you would have if you actually achieved your goal.

It was very easy for me to have a burning desire for life when I was unsure of the outcome of my medical tests. I had a burning desire. "I want to live," was my battle cry. You can be sure I was putting emotion behind those words.

Once I knew I was going to live, I had to figure out how I could create that burning desire every day. I found that it was about knowing the most important thing to do and nothing else. It had to be a focus so strong and clear that no one or nothing could get in the way of what I had to do. Knowing what you want in your life through knowing your purpose and your values will bring you that kind of passion or burning desire.

How to create it:

Step 1
At the end of each day, write down six things that you absolutely have to do the next day. The number can be less if your projects are large. Prioritize the tasks according to their importance on a full-size sheet of paper, leaving space between each item.

Step 2
Underline the name of each project, and under each project name, list all the steps that need to be done in order to accomplish that project.

What might happen by doing this?
As an example, you might be less likely to talk too long during a phone conversation or with a work associate. The other person might find this strange if you have been a chatterer up until now. Tell him you are trying some new techniques for making your life more productive and happy and that you are trying to complete your tasks quickly. The other person may not be too happy with the new you, so you might want to share with him the ideas of this chapter.

PRINCIPLE TWO
Energy fuels focus.

It's important to manage your energy. If you have no energy, not a lot happens for you. It's impossible to connect with others in a deep way. Energy helps us connect. Energy is even more important than time management. It's the energy you bring to a project that produces the ideal results.

Using words associated with the Very High Life-View of Self will make you feel very good and lead to a healthier, happier and more successful life. On the other hand, words from the Very Low Life-View of Self will zap your energy and lower your emotions, which is never good. Low emotions lower your immune system and can lead to poor health.

In each column below, note the words that make you feel really good and the ones that make you feel very bad. Write them down in your journal and express how each word makes you feel. What are you doing when you feel this way?

VERY LOW Life-View of Self	VERY HIGH Life-View of Self
Misery	Bliss/Joy
Shame	Serenity
Guilt	Love
Hopelessness	Forgiveness
Fear	Optimism
Pride	Trust
LOW Life-View of Self	**HIGH Life-View of Self**
Humiliation	Acceptance
Blame	Willingness
Regret	Reason
Anxiety	Understanding
Scorn	Satisfaction

Your burning desire is a unique creator of energy and fuels your focus in the direction of your desires.

How do you create a burning desire?

Step 1

Determine what you are feeling when you get up each morning by looking at the lists of words above, then writing down the first word that comes to mind in your Daytimer™, Palm Pilot™ or journal.

Step 2

Ask yourself how much you are enjoying the project or responsibilities you are handling with your job. Again, write the first word that comes to mind, noting whether it is positive or negative.

Step 3

Ask yourself whether you are living your life for yourself or for others. How does that make you feel? Write it down, noting a positive or negative response.

Step 4

Ask yourself why you are at your current job. Because of the benefits? Friends? A lack of credentials?

Step 5

Repeat the previous step with each of your significant relationships.

What else should you become aware of?

- Become aware of how you're feeling so you can adjust your feelings to a more positive experience. This can bring you better health and better feelings of self-worth.
- Positive feelings are always more encouraging than negative feelings. Catch yourself during a negative moment.
- Become aware of what you're thinking when presenting information to a client or manager. Positive and negative feelings give different messages. What messages are you delivering today, each moment, to your spouse, special friends and children?
- Manage your energy because it is the power of life.

PRINCIPLE THREE
Positive self-talk can create a positive reality.

This principle segues nicely from the previous principle concerning energy. Did you know, for instance, that each of us has 60,000 thoughts spanning today, yesterday and the day before yesterday? If you don't monitor your thoughts, they will end up creating your life for you. Pay attention to what your mind's voice is saying.

Have you ever caught yourself saying things like:

"Boy, what a loser I must be."

"Why can't I ever do it right?"

"Dad said I wasn't tall enough or strong enough to make the first team."

"I'm stupid."

"I don't make enough money."

"I'm not good enough."

"What a pain in the neck I must be."

If you haven't used any of these phrases, think of the ones you do use. Write them in your journal now.

Can you really identify with these negative statements? Could you change them to something more positive? Look at the feelings from

Principle 2. Pay attention to your words when you find yourself talking negatively. Identify what positive feelings you could have.

Actions to enhance greater awareness of your self-talk:

Step 1

Catch yourself when you hear a negative thought. Create a mantra that goes something like this: "Whoops! The new (insert your name) is going to say (rephrase the negative thought into something positive).

Step 2

If you are in your office or home most of the day, get two containers (vases, glasses, cups) and place small items such as marbles, paper clips or beads into one of the containers. Every time you catch yourself having a negative thought throughout the day, use your new mantra and put a bead into the other container. At the end of the day, look at all negative thoughts you have caught. Within two or three weeks, you'll find that you're having fewer negative thoughts. Don't get disappointed too soon and quit.

Step 3

If you spend a lot of time in your car each day, then try this one. Stretch a rubber band around your hand. When you catch yourself having a negative feeling, say your mantra and snap yourself with the rubber band. At the end of the day, look at your wrist to see if you have some red dots there, or think about how many times you have snapped yourself.

Step 4

As you catch your negative thoughts and substitute more and more positive ones, begin writing affirmations that you believe describe a better way of living. Examples of affirmations are:

- "I am getter slimmer and slimmer every day. Every part of my body is in alignment with the prototype of wholeness, every muscle, cell, bone, organ and tissue function according to the blueprint of infinite perfection. I personify well being, and I feel great!"
- "I am promoted because of my great talents, experience and work ethic."
- "I am amply rewarded for the work I give. This work allows me to express my talents and knowledge in ways that bring me satisfaction and financial gain, that amply meet my needs, with plenty to share and to spare."

- "I am healthy, energetic and filled with strength and great vitality. Every part of my body radiates the glow of well being.
- "My relationship with my (spouse, boss, co-workers, children) is getting better and better."
- "I am receiving enough abundance to happily satisfy all my debt, put away for retirement, put away for my child's college and still have enough to play and have fun."

You might even come up with affirmations that incorporate some of your work goals:

- "I am boosting my employees' attitudes in such a way we all share in an increase of (X number) percent of the great profits we are making."
- "I am getting (X number) phone calls about my products/services. Everyone wants what I sell. Everyone wants to pay my full asking price. They are happy to see me and easily sign my contract."
- "I am traveling to Hong Kong with enough money from my bonus to easily afford it and have a great time while also learning from such a rich culture."

Step 5
Say these affirmations out loud with enthusiasm and emotion every day for ten to fifteen minutes, on the rides to and from work. Say them any time you are free to voice them aloud and from a place of good feeling. It will make you feel so good.

Step 6
Take the previous step one step further. Record your words with music in the background for about ten minutes. Pop the tape into your cassette player on the way to work and repeat your words along with the cassette.

What are you purposefully doing?

- You're being specific. You're focused on the positive.
- When you say them with feeling—knowing that they will happen or that you don't care one way or the other—you will be surprised at how quickly they arrive.

One person I worked with, Marcie, with wanted success so much that she decided to try this principle. She told her husband what she was going to do to get what she wanted. He laughed at her. So never tell anyone what you want if you know he will be negative out of jealousy or ignorance. Thank heaven, Marcie did it anyway. Within one year, she achieved what she had wanted in her five-year dream plan.

I did this one myself, and my abundance became apparent within a month. I was so shocked and frightened by the strength and feeling of the recorded words and music that for several days I wouldn't say the affirmations, or listen to them, until I understood how they helped (I found I actually achieved things much more quickly). Now I create a monthly cassette tape of my affirmations to gain all that I wish for in my life. I get what I want more often than not.

Be careful not to hold on to feelings of want (the feeling that something is missing or lacking in your life) while using this principle because you may experience more want. Think of a time when you had a great success. Remember the feelings you associated with that time, and think about what you want now that's also associated with that feeling.

PRINCIPLE FOUR
Shape your reality through visualization.

If you have a business meeting planned two weeks from now, you are probably wondering many things, such as who is going to attend, what their hot buttons are, what their attitudes might be, what objections they might have, what outcome might occur. Did you realize that just by visualizing this meeting ahead of time, you are actually creating a more successful outcome?

When the day of the meeting occurs you won't be surprised at who is or is not present, and you won't leave the meeting thinking you were at a disadvantage about anything because you already considered many different outcomes. Visualizing is an excellent tool for creating what you want to happen.

What if I told you that competitive horseback riders uses this technique? Would you be shocked? Before any good rider goes into the ring, she gets notes from the judge as to what the judge expects to see. Then the rider visualizes exactly what will happen, how it will feel and how it will look. Olympians and world-class tennis players such as Martina Navratilova, Andre Agassi and Monica Seles also do this regularly.

James E. Loehr, who is recognized worldwide for his pioneering research in peak performance and mental toughness of athletes, calls visualization the "ideal performance state." It is the state of emotional control that allows each of us to perform at his best, regardless of circumstances. (Mr. Loehr's credentials are extensive. Because of this, he is paid more than a hundred thousand dollars to work with another kind of performer—the business executive.)

Laura Wilkinson, a gold medallist in diving at the 2000 Olympics in Sydney, also used visualization to create success. Just six months prior to the ten-meter platform dive competition, Wilkinson broke three bones in her foot. During practice for the Olympics, she used mental imagery, because she could not physically endure the practice. Instead, every day, she envisioned the competition and felt what it would be like to stand in front of thousands of people. She imagined her excitement, the feelings in her muscles, everything it would take to create the winning dive.

PRINCIPLE FIVE
Decluttering the space around you allows more energy to come to you.

Decluttering is a key aspect of the ancient Chinese practice called feng shui, which dates back to the Song Dynasty. In 1988, a Neolithic grave site was excavated in the Henan province, which revealed that ancient people were practicing some form of feng shui about 6,000 years ago. This is not a New Age tool or one to be fearful of using. Rather, it is an ancient truth that allows more success to come to you.

Have you ever cleaned out your closet only to get a gift of clothing or shoes soon after? I have. Several years ago, I really took charge of my closet and got rid of things I hadn't worn for three years or more. On a trip to visit my mother shortly thereafter, she wanted to go shopping and ended up buying me three suits for work.

Recently, I cleared out shoes that I hadn't worn in years. Two weeks later, on a consulting assignment in Connecticut, a client asked me to help select some appropriate interview clothing at Nordstrom's. I walked in to find a boot sale going on. I ended up buying three pairs, which all together were less expensive than the one pair of boots or shoes that I would normally have purchased.

The same formula works for your office. Clean up the space around your desk. Get rid of files that you are not working on right now. I usually get a lot of resistance to this. For example, Cathy, the sales person I spoke of earlier in the chapter, decided to go into her office on a Saturday. When she arrived, she had to make decisions about what to keep and what not to keep. She said that at first it was hard to decide, but as the process went along, it became very easy. She was eager to throw away what wasn't needed.

She got rid of old, out-of-date files, three-year-old newspapers and magazines she thought she would read if she ever had the time, half-empty soda cans and so on. She washed away food and drink residue and polished her desk.

Cathy also added a live plant that acted as a magnet to draw chi' (energy) into her work space and a mirror on top of her computer so she could see who was approaching since her back was to the door. (Mirrors can also make a business more profitable because they symbolically double everything they reflect.) Cathy told me she stood back and appraised her five hours' worth of effort and was delighted with the change. She said she didn't feel so overburdened or overwhelmed with so much stuff surrounding her.

The following Monday morning, her many associates arrived, saw her desk and surrounding areas and assumed she had been fired. Upon closer attention, family pictures were spotted on one shelf. They knew something had happened, albeit not a firing. And in less than four months, Cathy went from being the number ten sales person to number four.

What might occur:
- Get rid of the clutter so more will come to you.
- Apply feng shui to many aspects of your life, both professional and personal.

Another example of how this works occurred with Pia, another client of mine. She was about to go on vacation but had eleven stacks of paperwork on her desk, which represented her most important customers' files. I challenged her to put them into expandable files, write down the name of every item she included in the file and put them away in a filing cabinet. Ultimately, she did so with great reservation.

Lucky Pia! The first day she was on vacation, the person who was to partner with her during her absence received a phone call from one of her very important clients. The item being requested was found within sixty seconds. A very relieved helper reported this to Pia, who continues using this system and has since been promoted to a level of accounts handled only by the best sales executives.

The latter story also is one of time management. According to time management gurus, most people lose up to an hour a week looking for lost items at work. By using this expandable files method and writing down everything you put into the files, you, too, will gain more time to get real work done.

Pia not only got paperwork off her desk in an efficient manner, she removed the clutter and gained more than an hour a week that had previously been spent looking for lost things.

What might occur if you do this action:
- Open space is created.
- Overwhelming feelings do not occur.
- The list of work to be completed for the next day is simply written.
- Allow a project line for important things that need to be done for yourself and/or family.
- It clears your mind and puts an end to the work day.
- You feel refreshed at the end of the day rather than distracted.
- You sleep better.
- Waking up and worrying for an hour or two in the middle of the night is useless and disturbing. Most times, actually performing the project you're so worried about will only take a brief amount time.

If you want to create more success in your business life, then create a better office space:

Step 1
Never place your important files on the floor, no matter how busy you are or how cluttered you office gets. If your files get stepped on, extremely negative energy is created that affects your work.

Step 2
Never allow your important files to be placed under your desk or table. This creates the same negative effect.

Step 3
Never place any important files, or even filing cabinets, under staircases. Again, it creates extremely negative energy that affects your work.

Step 4
Never place files next to a bathroom wall.

Step 5
After you have put your papers into expandable files, make a list of everything you placed inside the file and put the list where you can find it easily. Eventually, when you have some time on your hands, you can decide what to do with the contents. Simply cross off what you take out or throw away. You can reuse an expandable file by writing on the other side of it.

The ideas expressed above will help keep you working at peak performance. What is peak performance? Think about it for a moment. How do you perform the day before you go on vacation? If you could do this more often, look at what you would achieve in the work arena alone.

PRINCIPLE SIX
The written word can lead to a manifest reality.

Here are some wonderful books I encourage you to read.

Write It Down, Make It Happen (Harriette Anne Klauser, 2000)

The Magic of Thinking Big (David J. Schwartz, Ph.D., 1958)

The Magic of Believing, The Science of Reaching your Goal (Claude M. Bristol, 1948).

These books not only prove that the power of the written word is not a new concept but that it is also a science.

I experienced this when I was going to regular doctors' appointments and chemo treatments. I used the time to write and create what I wanted for my life. I got to know other patients at the time who were doing poorly with their treatments. They would talk to me for hours trying to find out my secrets for handling my own treatments so well. They were often embarrassed because they would take up so much of my time, forgetting that I, too, was a patient.

Create a life you really want:

Step 1
Set up a schedule for keeping a journal at a specific time each day. (Remember, a deliberate plan must be followed every day. What follows is my plan; what will your routine be like?)

Step 2
Write as if your day has already happened. For example, I used to write every morning before going to work, pretending that it was 10 p.m. and that I was ready for bed. I would visualize my day already happening and list the many calls from excited users of my services, all eagerly booking me for events in the near future and agreeing to my fee, with no concern about how they were going to pay me for my services.

Step 3
Write as if it were a year from now. What date would that be? This doesn't have to be something you start on New Year's day either. You

can start today. Begin with, "I am sitting in my new red car I only dreamed about a year ago. Today is June 30." (make the date on year from now)

Step 4

Never think about grammar, verb tense or spelling. When you write, it must feel good. Do not have an outcome. In other words, have an attitude of, "It's just got to happen." Write for the love of creating rather than love of what you are getting (outcome).

Step 5

Write a fairy tale in which you are the star creating the life you desire. When I do this, I write it as a dream plan, as if it were five years from now. Then I write down the things I will want to do three years from now in order to get to that point. Finally, I write my one-year plan, which is basically a list of things I need to do to get to what I want in three and five years. I love this technique and use it often, changing my mind on some points, to adapt to the changes of real life.

What might occur by doing this?

- Writing begins to bring about results in only two or three weeks.
- Perhaps you've been living your life by doing everything everyone tells you to do. "You must do this. You must do that." Finally, you are whirling out of control on the fast-paced merry-go-round called life. Writing down your vision for the future will help you get control of what you're doing and get clear about your own purpose for life. A better life can be created by capturing all the negative thoughts that go unnoticed in your head.
- A few years ago, Oprah Winfrey talked about keeping a gratitude journal. I found that this technique changes your thinking from negative to positive. The more you write about things you're grateful for, the more often you are positive, and the more you allow positive feelings into your life. Check your feelings as you list in your journal the things for which you are grateful. It is an easy way to change your world forever because you are relaxing and letting only good thoughts and feelings into your being.
- You will sometimes get exactly what you write about. So start writing now! If you don't take time to dream or plan, you'll just keep on getting what you have been getting day after day.

When you are willing to make some dramatic changes, life will change for the better. Don't wait for an illness or other life-challenging event to realize how effective this principle can be!

- Although it is somewhat difficult to get started, just keep your pen moving for fifteen minutes or longer. Thirty minutes are all you need to create a five-year plan. If you want, you can even wait a day to do your three-year plan.
- You must make decisions about what you want for your life. Most people actually spend more time planning their vacations than planning their lives. No wonder our vacations turn out so well! You don't show up at the airport and ask the sky captain, "I'm on vacation now, where should I go?" No, you must make a deliberate plan, just as you must make a plan for your life.
- Ask how well you know yourself. After all, it's called "self-esteem," not "other-esteem." The voices in your head that tell you you're not good enough might just cease and desist when you know more about yourself.

PRINCIPLE SEVEN
Good nutrition and exercise will result in self-confidence, energy and great health.

Just before my life was about to change forever (as I feared, because I had to take some powerful drugs designed for breast cancer patients), I received a call from a woman named Julie. She said, "Marilyn, I'm a runner. I have run marathons throughout this treatment process. You can do it." "But, Julie, I'm not a runner," I told her. But my mind triggered another thought: "I can do it, Julie. I'm not a runner, but I am a walker, and I will walk through this entire ordeal. I can do that. I just know I can." It was the greatest commitment I ever made to myself. It helped me set a deliberate plan, create momentum and gain vitality and energy.

First thing every morning, I would lie in bed, doing what I called a body scan. "Does anything burn or hurt? Or am I okay?" I would then bypass the kitchen, avoiding any bad or negative news, avoiding caffeine and advancing to my corner of the world that I called "my healing sanctuary."

I believe everyone can and should move first thing in the morning. You can dance to your favorite tunes, stretch, jump up and down, do Pilates or lift weights—even if its for just ten minutes. Doing any kind of movement in the morning can help build your confidence in all areas of your life.

I believe that if you don't have time for exercise, you don't grow; and if you don't grow, you die. Wayne Dyer, Ph.D., author, speaker and a teacher of mine says, "If you don't take time for exercise now, you will later by being sick."

Here are a few other ways you can improve your health and your life:

Step 1
Look into eating more nutritionally to balance out the highs and lows of energy. Keep a food journal. It was the best thing I could have done to jump-start my better eating habits.

Step 2
What are you tolerating in your life, nutritionally? Be honest with yourself. No one else is going to read your journal. Determine if your intake of caffeine, sweets and/or processed foods is causing your weight gain.

Step 3
What are you tolerating in your life in terms of your activities—no social life, no exercise, working too many hours, spending too much time in front of the boob tub or in Internet chat rooms? Are you spending all your evenings running children to events and doing chores instead of being with your children? Are you hanging around negative people and letting them drain you? Are you going to bed too late each evening? Are you taking everything away from yourself only to give, give, give to others?

Step 4
Don't you just hate it when someone tells you how much water you must drink in order to be healthy? I felt that way for years, but I now understand how much it heals and makes my life so much healthier.

Think of drinking water this way: If I have to drink sixty-four ounces of water a day, anything less than that doesn't create a healthy body, because it's only above sixty-four ounces that you rid your body of toxins that might be creating ill health.

Did you know certain Native American medicine men used only water to heal their people? They would have the sick person continuously drink water until he started feeling better. When I first heard of this, I was having a difficult time believing it. But then my dear friend Pat Miceli-Sundin mentioned that she was familiar with the practice. I was shocked. I had figured she would scoff at the notion, but instead, she told me a story about her experiences with Outward Bound. As she and her buddies were trekking up a mountain, the air got thinner, and Pat developed a migraine headache, something she'd never had before. Her group waited while she drank a gallon of water. By the time she finished drinking the water, the migraine was gone!

Here's what can happen when you put this information into practice:
- You'll enjoy a healthier lifestyle (for life, not just a month).
- You'll have more energy to give to the things that matter most in your life.
- You'll have more confidence.
- You'll enjoy longevity by practicing your good habits daily.

Three final ideas that will bring more success to you in both your professional and personal lives:

Multitasking can bring you more satisfaction. Recent studies show that when multitasking, one is unable to do the best job possible, only a mediocre job. Take one item at a time and thoroughly analyze it; then decide what needs to be done and do it!

Really take time to listen. Listen to the words and pay attention to the body language of the person speaking. A child can tell when you really aren't listening; so can the "adult child" (your boss, peer, friends). Stop thinking about other things when you pick up the phone. If you can't put those things out of your mind, don't pick the phone up if the caller is someone who matters to you even slightly.

Finally, really get to know yourself inside and out. Know what you care about. Understand what drives you. Control your thoughts. Figure out the most important things you desire in life. If you have a spouse and children, this would be an excellent opportunity to plan together. When you know yourself thoroughly, you will have developed values, which can allow you to speak out about what you need and not feel guilty about it. You'll free yourself from guilt by doing for yourself first.

Marilyn Schott

Formerly a highly successful Senior Vice President of Coldwell Banker Commercial Real Estate Company in Cincinnati, Ohio, and Vice President and General Manager of a firm in which she managed over a million square feet of public warehousing, Marilyn has taken her entrepreneurial knowledge of building multi-million dollar businesses into corporate America with her speaking and training business. With previous modeling and television background, she is quickly becoming one of America's most sought-after speaker and trainer in human potential. Since 1992 Marilyn has been a member of National Speakers Association and through this organization is a Certified Speaking Professional (CSP) Candidate for 2004. She serves as a board member for NSA-Central Florida. Marilyn speaks on *How To Be Memorable Through Attire, Vocal Variety* and *Gestures and Scripting*. In addition, she teaches the principles of *Managing Your Energy to Engage the Full Potential of Every Day*. These topics can be developed for customer service, career strategy, leadership and speaking and facilitation skills for Fortune 500 executives, sales executives, entrepreneurs, financial planners, bankers, CPAs, physicians and people who desire to be in the media. Her clients include American Express Financial Services, Merrill Lynch, Procter & Gamble, Kellogg, U. S. Precision Lens, Federal Reserve Bank, Anthem East, Anthem Midwest, Anthem Prescription and Comcast. Marilyn's mission to all she meets is "To Educate. To Energize. To Inspire. To Transform." She is a wife to Joe, mother to Becky, a breast cancer survivor, and Mummy to her 8-pound Maltese puppy, Sophia Sabrina Schott.

Marilyn Schott
Marilyn Schott, LLC
2110 Tocobaga Lane
Nokomis, FL 34275-5313
(941) 412-3100, Office
(941) 412-3300, Fax
Email: email@MarilynSchott.com
www.MarilynSchott.com